Christian Ethics

Christian Ethics

VICTOR LEE AUSTIN

B L O O M S B U R Y

LONDON · NEW DELHI · NEW YORK · SYDNEY

Bloomsbury T&T Clark

An imprint of Bloomsbury Publishing Plc

50 Bedford Square   175 Fifth Avenue
London   New York
WC1B 3DP   NY 10010
UK   USA

www.bloomsbury.com

First published 2012

British Library Cataloguing-in-Publication Data
A catalogue record for this books is available from the British Library.

ISBN: HB: 978-0-567-03219-5
PB: 978-0-567-03220-1

Typeset by Fakenham Prepress Solutions, Fakenham, Norfolk NR21 8NN
Printed and bound in Great Britain

In gratitude for my teachers
and the institutions that took me as a student:
St. John's College in Santa Fe
The General Theological Seminary
Fordham University

CONTENTS

ACKNOWLEDGMENTS

When Tom Kraft of T & T Clark asked me to contribute this volume to the Guides for the Perplexed series, I eagerly embraced this project as an opportunity to put into words an understanding of the subject that, over a couple of decades of study and teaching, has gradually commended itself to me. At that time I had recently completed a term as an adjunct professor in Christian ethics at the General Theological Seminary, and earlier I had taught ethics at various colleges, including Mount Aloysius in Cresson, Pennsylvania. There is nothing like teaching a subject for exposing its depths and one's own ignorance. And conversely: when I seek to understand something, the challenge of teaching it is an irreplaceable opportunity. But now I know something else: the further opportunity to follow teaching with writing a Guide to the subject. It is good to ponder, good to teach, good to write. And so, first of all, I give thanks to my students, to the schools that have had me as a teacher, and to my editor and publisher.

This book makes the case that ethics is about living together as friends. And no author could write without having the friendship of readers. I am grateful to a number of colleagues who read this manuscript in earlier forms, in part or in whole: David Cloutier, James Cornwell, Joel Daniels, Susan Ironside, and Bill Mattison. They are, of course, not responsible for my failure to learn from them as much as I should have.

Once again it is a pleasure to own my debt to the Reverend Andrew C. Mead, rector of Saint Thomas Church, who invited me to be the parish's first theologian-in-residence. At Saint Thomas I am able to offer adult theology classes that are aimed at a serious level, and that are welcome and supported broadly. This manifests Father Mead's own commitment to the pastoral importance of doctrine and lively teaching; and for him and for the parish I have deep thanks.

Most of all, I wish to thank my teachers. And who are they? At St. John's College in New Mexico, the professors are all called "tutors" and done so without distinction of rank. This is because the school recognizes its true teachers as the texts themselves, the Great Books, which readers are to approach with neither undue reverence nor excessive skepticism. Thus I learned, in those formative years of early adulthood, that at best I could become only a more advanced reader; and to this day, at the beginning of a course of study, I will tell my students that I am only that, only, if you will, a guide. As a Christian, I believe that there is only one Teacher. But he works through many texts, many persons, many institutions. It is to those teachers and institutions that have particularly formed me that I dedicate this book.

New York City
December 2011

INTRODUCTION

I'M PERPLEXED; AREN'T YOU?

Perplexity in the matter of Christian ethics should neither surprise nor distress us. For ethics has to do with how we humans live in the broadest sense: how we live *as humans*. Just about every other subject is a narrowing-down compared with ethics. Long ago, I taught mathematics to Pueblo Indians in the American Southwest. My job, and my concern, ranged from basic accuracy in computation to engendering some of the joy and beauty that is displayed in numbers. My job concerned the human good insofar as mathematics is part of that good. But questions of politics and justice, of the best way to live one's life—questions that, in my students' case, would range from intermarriage with Indians of another tribe, to alcohol and gambling, to doubts about the perpetuation of their own religious traditions in the face of modernity—these questions were put aside in the mathematics classroom. They were left outside the door. And necessarily so: if one does not acquire basic mathematical literacy, one's flourishing is thereby limited.

But in the face of ethics no doors are closed, no subjects excluded from consideration. Students of ethics are like novice swimmers pushed immediately into the deep end of the swimming pool, forced to thrash about and keep our wits in the midst of quite a mess of things all about us. It is no wonder we are confused. Ethics, it seems to me, is the most perplexing of subjects.

What this book offers is not a comprehensive set of answers to ethical questions. It will not tell you what to do about your sex life, or what to do if you see money on the floor, or how to operate a business ethically. Rather, this book will invite you to consider some of the basic questions of ethics, including the question of what difference it makes to speak of *Christian* ethics. This book aims to have an inviting style, and its author stands before you not as the Answer Man but as a Guide. Frankly, sometimes he's rather perplexed himself. But, as a guide, he can assure you that he has been here before, that he has himself taken on these questions and worked through them and found the process helpful in coming to a better grasp of what it means to live a life that is humanly worth living.

Here is the path that is in front of you, should you choose to continue to read this Guide.

When we first plunge into taking ethics seriously, we find that there is a lot of resistance to doing so. Many voices will tell us that ethics is not a real subject (unlike mathematics!). Sometimes they say that there is no such thing as right or wrong; at other times they say that everything is relative or subjective. So the first chapter takes up these claims, examines them, and shows reasons why they fall short. Ethics really is something that we can explore with our reason. In making this argument, Chapter 1 also makes the theological point, that Christian faith has a concern to be reasonable and to defend reason.

But what, then, is Christian about Christian ethics? Chapter 2 explores several possibilities, including those given by the place of the Bible in moral reflection, the rules or laws that we find in the Bible, and the inescapability of narrative. The argument pivots on the particular character of the Christian narrative, especially its claim of universalizability by virtue of Jesus' transcendence (it will say that he, the one fully human being, is a character in a narrative who is at one with the author). The chapter concludes with the paradox that Christian ethics is in the end just ethics, in that its concern is the flourishing of all human beings as such.

The third chapter lays out three alternatives for the big picture of human flourishing. The first is that we flourish by obeying such commands as are laid upon us, whether by our rational nature itself or from outside (say, by divine command). This is the ethics of duty, often termed "deontological." The second is an opposing claim, that there are no duties laid upon us that could not be overridden by outcome-considerations. For, on this second view, the heart of morality is to bring about as much good as we can. This ethics of outcome is often called "utilitarianism." The chapter shows the strengths of both views and illustrates theological versions of each.

At the end it lays out a third alternative, the ethics of virtue, and with a sports analogy suggests that any truly human ethic must have (a) exceptionless rules that lay out boundary conditions, (b) a concern for the outcome of human action, but also (c) an interest in the development of excellence in human character. Indeed, it will be said, human excellence is the overriding consideration, although it cannot exist without the earlier two considerations (of rules and outcomes).

Chapters 4 and 5 expand upon human virtues. In a line of thinking that, while eclectic, draws much from Aquinas, Chapter 4 looks into the oddness of the word "good" and then what possibly might be meant by "the human good." With a broad answer, it proceeds to set forth the moral virtues whereby we are able to carry out our projects over time and to live together with one another. Chapter 5 continues with the question of how we make good judgments. It's not just a matter of following our conscience (for our conscience, it will be said, is nothing other than our own coming to a judgment about action). We need an excellence of character that's called "good sense," but even more (and here the Christian contribution to our study becomes quite direct) we need gifts from God, particularly the theological virtues of faith, hope, and love. There are some strongly theological questions here, and this Guide does not shy away from pointing them out: the relation of God's gifts (grace) to human free choice, for instance.

The final two chapters take up questions that are not customarily thought of in terms of an overview of Christian ethics, and yet they are essential to a right understanding.

The first is friendship. Friendship is an essential topic to Christian ethics for two reasons. The first is that, from Aristotle on, it has been the capstone of moral discourse. Friendship has a high place in Aristotle's book on ethics. And in my experience, students intuitively grasp that the point of living morally should be that we are able to live with one another as friends. Second, there is a reason that derives from the Christian claim that God gives the virtue of love. This virtue may be defined, as Aquinas boldly says, as friendship with God—and thereby, friendship with God's friends. So everything about us as human beings is, in the end, aimed at making us capable of living with one another in the common life of friendship. There are many questions raised by this view, from certain suspicions of friendship raised in the Bible, to the matter of our finitude: how many friends can we really have? But they are questions worth the exploration.

Chapter 7 sets itself up by raising the question that disability poses to a virtue ethics. If the point of all this is to flourish as human beings, what about those who cannot do so, not only physically but particularly mentally? Here the Guide takes up the very odd notion of "person" and, looking at it both as an ancient word and as a theological word, sketches a way to ground fundamental human equality that is neither simply in the future nor merely individualistic. It turns out that the fact that we are persons implicates everything that has come before: our nature, our good, how we succeed at being human, the various virtues or excellences, and particularly the necessity and goal of friendship.

Almost no particular moral question will be answered by this Guide. And every chapter in it could open out into volumes of further inquiry. In this regard, the reader may find helpful the notes for further reading at the end of each chapter. That there are such notes indicates that this Guide will not, and cannot, eliminate all perplexities. But its author, having himself struggled in the deep end of the swimming pool on many an occasion, hopes that his readers will in the end find their perplexities diminished. We can ask these questions, and in doing so, see better what we are about as human beings. Christian ethics, in the end, is about all of us being successful as human beings.

CHAPTER ONE

Can We Talk?

Why some people argue that ethics cannot be the subject of rational discourse, and how such arguments can be answered

Challenges to the Reasonableness of Ethics

I start with an observation. Most people have a sense of right and wrong. When we think about things we've done, sometimes we judge that we have done what we ought not to have done, and as a result we may feel guilt. "I was driving along, listening to the radio, when I pulled right in front of that bicyclist. I ought to have seen him before I moved into the turn lane." And at other times, we may judge that we have done something ethically commendable, and as a result we may feel happy about ourselves. "I was on my way to play cards when she phoned with news of her mother's diagnosis. Of course I went right to the hospital. It was good to be with them."

This sense of right and wrong that we apply introspectively, we also apply to others. I might judge that *you* have done morally well, or that you have fallen morally short. And I might do the same about *him* or *her* or *them*, and about individuals or groups. We formulate moral judgments in all three grammatical persons, and in both singular and plural.

And yet, particularly when it comes to others, many people today are likely to hesitate in such judgments. I might be ignorant of some significant details of the situation, so how dare I say that what was done was right or wrong? Alternately, that person might have a different sense of morality than I do, and I should not force my own morals upon him. And in "I—you" situations, I might hesitate to judge you lest it harm our relationship with one another.

So on the one hand, most people have some sense of ethics, a sense of right and wrong. And yet most people also know that the matter is complicated, to the extent that we often withhold making judgments upon others. How can this tension be resolved?

For a number of people, the tension is resolved by denying that ethics is a proper topic for rational discourse. They may say that our sense of right and wrong is nothing more than an illusion, something we need to grow out of (as we grow out of our childhood sense that the sun circles over the earth every day and our childhood sense that our parents are God). Ethics on this view is just a sophisticated way, and perhaps a deceptive and manipulative way, of expressing personal preferences. Or it may be that our sense of right and wrong has no bearing upon reality because we are overwhelmingly determined in our actions by factors outside our control—which is to say that, according to this view, we lack freedom to accomplish ethically meaningful action.

Yet another way to resolve the tension is to grant that it is meaningful to speak of ethics but only within given cultural contexts. In a Western European democracy in the early twenty-first century, say, such-and-such activity is morally right, but in other cultures at other times it could well be morally wrong. Thus when faced with the differing judgments made upon collecting interest on money, or the differing judgments made upon polygamous sexual relations, or any other matter upon which cultures have differed, the most we can say is that what's right and wrong simply depends on the cultural context. On this view, it would be illusory to think, for instance, that honesty is really and in itself commendable, because "honesty is commendable" means only that it is deemed commendable in certain contexts.

Now if any of these strategies is true—if the tension we feel between our sense of ethical right and wrong, on the one hand, and difficulties of making judgments, on the other, must be resolved by making ethics out to be in some fundamental way a disguise—then clearly there is nothing to talk about in this book. For if ethics is just a mask for something else (the imposition of will, say), then there is no point in our troubling our minds about ethics, and this Guide for the perplexed is already a much longer book than it should be.

Yet to resolve the tension by saying that ethics is just camouflage may not seem satisfactory. If I failed, as a driver, to take proper precautions and as a result a bicyclist ran into me, is the corresponding sense that I acted in a morally wrong way really an illusion? If, on the other hand, I changed plans in order to be with a needy friend and her mother, is the corresponding sense that I acted in a morally right way also illusory?

I believe that there are good reasons to reject the strategies that deny the reality of ethics. In the main part of this chapter, I will outline some principal objections to ethics and some reasons not to accept those objections. Readers may then decide if it's worth their while to continue with the rest of the book. My over-arching argument is that before we can talk about Christian ethics, we need to satisfy ourselves that "ethics" is something with enough claim upon reality to command our attention. Because the sentiments against it are so strong in contemporary Western cultures, those of us who are in one of those cultures need to know the countering arguments. But do not think that, when it looks at the reasonableness of speaking about ethics, this chapter is putting theology on hold, bracketing it aside for later consideration. On the contrary: for Christian theology the defense of reason is fundamental—a claim that I will unpack in the final section of this chapter.

First Challenge: There's No Such Thing as Moral Right and Wrong

It is clear that moral judgments of right and wrong are different than other sorts of claims we might make. To say that Paris is the capital of France or that water is constituted of oxygen and hydrogen is to make a different kind of claim than that Joe ought not to have killed Josephine or that Samantha did a good thing by standing up to the school bully. Although it is difficult to describe the difference between these two kinds of claims—one might say the first is "factual" and the latter not, although, in the case of water, it's a pretty sophisticated line of reasoning that one has to follow before one gets to the fact of its being H_2O—still it is clear that there is some sort of difference here. And so, it seems, one might say that morality is unreal on the grounds that moral claims are not "factual." We can't live very well as human beings without Paris, without geography, without politics, and so forth, nor can we live intelligently without the truths of chemistry. But perhaps we could get along without all our moral problems if we just recognized that morality isn't real.

This first challenge is the most radical approach to the problem: to deny altogether that there is anything real to morality. Here are two main headings under which such an argument is sometimes made.

Amoralism is the view that there just is no such thing as right and wrong. Amoralists are people who try to live accordingly without morality. If right and wrong are merely illusions, then we should reject any impositions upon our life that come from others telling us, or even ourselves telling ourselves, that we ought to do certain things and we ought not to do other things.

Emotivism, often linked with amoralism, is the ethical theory that when we say something is right or wrong we are expressing our own emotional attitude towards it. Morality is not a judgment about actions, but rather an expression of our emotions. And when we express our emotions by declaring something right or wrong, we are at the same time attempting to entice others to adopt the same attitude for themselves. So if I say to my son that punching the nose of his little sister is "wrong," what I mean, according to emotivism, is (a) I don't like him punching the nose of his little sister, and (b) I want it to be that he, my son, doesn't like it either. "Ethical judgments are social instruments," concluded the American philosopher Charles L. Stevenson in an influential 1937 paper.[1]

When I teach ethics at college, there are usually a few students who find the amoralist or emotivist argument convincing, and many more who would like to find it convincing. They want to believe that morality is an illusion, and they are thus willing to consider that it flat out does not exist. But a simple experiment disabuses them. I will announce, say, that I intend to assign the final grades in the course on the basis of the length of their last names—those with the shorter names getting the higher grades. There will be outrage. "That's not fair!" Well, I say, what do you mean? "It's not right!" To which I might say, "But it's good for people to have shorter names—by which I mean that I like shorter names and you should too." And they then predictably say, "No, that's not right," and again try to invoke some notion of objective fairness.... . When you talk to students about their grades, amoralism and emotivism quickly flee away. I get absolutely nowhere with them by explaining that, since there is no such thing as right or wrong, all that matters is that one impose one's will successfully, and that it is my will to reward those who have shorter names with the better grades.

My students, in other words, find they are unwilling to abandon the idea that morality speaks to a feature of the world. When faced with an existentialist crisis over their grades, they discover that, after all, they hold "fairness" to be something real in the world about which we can and ought to have rational conversation. They thus discover the fundamental problem with amoralism. It is logically impossible to hold that everyone should be an amoralist.[2] For if I am willing for you to be an amoralist, then I am necessarily willing for you to do whatever you please. I am thus necessarily willing for you, if it pleases you, to deny me the right to be an amoralist. Which means, for example, that you could perfectly well use whatever is at your command to throw me in jail if I fail to act as you want me to act, and I would have no grounds for objection. If I were to say, "But there's no such thing as morality, therefore I should be able to do as I please," you could well reply, "There's no such thing as morality, therefore you have no grounds for objecting over what I do with you." Most amoralists really want everyone else to be moralists. My students think they would be happy amoralists, but they insist on denying that privilege to their teachers.

Second Challenge: There's No Such Thing as Freedom

A second challenge—*determinism*—runs like this. Judgments of moral right and wrong are meaningful only if the agent is free to do otherwise. But, in reality, our actions are determined and are not free. Therefore, since freedom is an illusion, so is morality.

Why might one think that freedom is an illusion? There are several possible lines of thought; I will limit myself to one that derives from our growth in the understanding of the human brain.

The more we know about how the brain works, the more it seems
that our thoughts and feelings are determined by the physical stuff
of our bodies. We have seen that attitudes and feelings can be
altered by the controlled introduction of pharmaceuticals. And we
feel that science is just at the threshold of an explosion of understanding of the brain—that, in another generation or two at most,
all sorts of mysteries about thought, memory, decision, intention,
fear, aggression, and so much else will be answered. We'll know
why we used to forget, and we won't forget any more. In the old
days (it will be said of benighted folk like you and me) we would
often do things that afterwards we felt bad about and couldn't
understand why we did them. "What were we thinking?" we used
to say. But now (in this future we envisage) we understand how our
brains give rise to intentions and how intentions give rise to action,
and there's no mystery any more. No mystery—and no freedom.[3]
Everything human is the result of chemicals at work in the human
body.

That, one might say, is science fiction, but such ideas exert
a powerful contemporary influence. For instance, Tom Wolfe's
best-selling novel *I Am Charlotte Simmons* is premised on the
basic question raised by neuroscience, the question of identity. Is
everything Charlotte believes and decides upon determined by her
brain functions? Is a human being to be identified with the matter
of which she is made? Or is there something more to being human,
more than our physicality?

The response to this second challenge may be introduced simply.
Each of us has the subjective experience of being free. If you ask me
if I had to write this book on Christian ethics, I will answer, "Of
course not." Did I have to include that reference to Tom Wolfe?
Not at all. There are many other things I could have done instead
of this book, and (once having taken on this book) many alternate
ways I could have written it. Having real options, and having
the power to act or not to act upon them, is fundamental to the
experience of being human. If we don't really have freedom, then
we are fundamentally deluded through our whole life.

Determinism—the view that freedom is illusory—cannot
account for a number of basic human experiences. If we were
to have a good talk with each other, you and I would each have
the sense of being listened to, of having our own views engaged,
and perhaps of leaving the conversation as persons different than

we were when we began it. But if there is no freedom, then our conversation (in Herbert McCabe's vivid image) is no different from two tape recorders running simultaneously.[4] *That*, of course, is what we mean when we say of a bad conversation, "We were just talking past each other." Human beings, and not tape recorders, are free.

So, I say, the response is simple. It is, however, unsatisfying, in that it leaves open many questions. Sometimes we *aren't* free (we might have been under the influence of drugs, or we might have been under the influence of a wicked stepmother, or we might have been simply ignorant of what was going on). Sometimes—perhaps most of the time—we are free only in certain respects. Given my age and my personal history up to this time, I am not free to become a ballet dancer. And I am not free to become you, whoever you are. I am Victor Lee Austin, and whatever I do will be in some fundamental continuity with what I have been and what I am. I am tempted to say that I am not free to become a woman (although that sort of change is, arguably, medically possible). Would you at least agree that I am not free to become an elephant—or an angel?

So freedom is limited in a number of ways. But to have something that's limited is not to have something that's extinguished. Limited freedom, freedom within parameters—freedom exercised under the influence of any number of things—is still real freedom. A good football (soccer) player cannot pick up the ball with his hands and throw it through a hoop and still call the game "football." Football is not basketball. Yet while he is limited within the rules and boundaries of what constitutes football, he at the same time might well be unlimited in the possibilities for being a good football player. He is free.

The defense of authentic human freedom is an important task for Christian ethics. Freedom and morality are inextricably connected.

Third Challenge: All Morality Is Subjective

The first and second challenges to the rationality of moral discourse were fundamental, in that they challenged the reality of morality as an object of discussion. As we turn to the third and fourth challenges—subjectivism and cultural relativism—we come to challenges that are less fundamental, and perhaps for that very reason more commonly accepted. Both subjectivism and cultural relativism hold that we are saying something true when we speak about morality. What they deny, however, is that there is any point to having a discussion about it. That is to say, on these views moral claims do point to something real, but it is an illusion to think that what they're pointing to is morality. And thus it makes no sense to try to have rational discourse about morality.

Moral subjectivism holds that a moral judgment is a claim about rightness or wrongness *according to the views of the person making the judgment.* In the subjectivist's view, moral judgments are not purported truths that have some standing independent of the person making the judgment. Rather, every moral judgment is founded upon the subject who makes the judgment. All moral judgments are thus *subjective.*

For instance, if I say that it is wrong to take home from the office a ream of copy paper and use it for my own purposes, I am indeed speaking a truth. But according to subjectivism, the truth is this: such an action does not accord with my own sense of morality. And according to subjectivism, that is the end of the story. I cannot go on to say, for instance, that there is a likelihood that my own sense of morality corresponds with something like justice that exists apart from me. That is to say, I cannot hold that my sense of justice is in accord with (or, conversely, might be at odds with) anything that's larger than I am.

Some writers consider emotivism to be a form of subjectivism, as it shares the claim that what matters is something within the person making the judgment. But for emotivism the important inner matter is the emotions (or perhaps the sheer will) of the subject. By contrast, above, I put emotivism alongside amoralism because it seems to me helpful to separate out and emphasize a certain dignity that lies with the subjectivist claim.

For although subjectivism denies that there is any point in trying to discuss it, the subjectivist view of morality upholds a proper correspondence between the moral judgments that an individual makes (upon actions and characters and the like) and the personal reality of the person making the judgments. This is, I deem, a fundamental truth of morality. The moral judgments I make correspond to the person I am. And why is that important?

It has to do with our sense that when we make moral decisions we reach into the depths of our character, into places where no other person has access, places where no one should attempt to interfere. True moral action must be free action; it cannot be coerced. We might say, in moral action we act according to our conscience.

The dignity that I see in moral subjectivism is that it is a theory used to respect and honor conscience. The subjectivist so highly values the importance of each person coming to his own decisions in matters of morality that he, the subjectivist, is unwilling to pass any unqualified judgments upon any decisions. He may make judgments, but in every case his judgments are qualified with such words as "according to my values" or "according to my sense of right and wrong."

This deference to the dignity of each person as a moral agent is commendable. But now I must also say it entails a mistake. And the mistake is easily seen if we introduce a third party.

Suppose Cheri takes home that ream of paper. You might say that it's wrong to steal from her employer, but you would probably qualify that judgment in accord with subjectivism: "According to my values, she shouldn't do that, but her values may be different. She may think her company rips off its employees all the time. I still wouldn't do it, but who am I to judge? It may be, according to her values, perfectly right for her to do that."

But now suppose you witness Cheri in the act of stealing a purse from a man on the street. Your first instinct might still be to say that, according to your values, she has done wrong, but her values are clearly different. I hope, however, that that would not be your first instinct. I hope your first instinct would be to defend the victim.

For there is a victim, and whenever there is a victim, there is an injustice that needs to be set right. It might not be your place to do so—although it might be! Perhaps you could interrupt the robbery. Or perhaps later you could confront your friend about her (yes) wrongful behavior. Or perhaps you should make a citizen's report to the authorities. Or, indeed, perhaps the circumstances are such that there is nothing for you to do. But you have seen it: you have seen that there is an injustice. And that's not just your subjective view.[5]

One way to put the difficulty with subjectivism is to say that it denies the reality of victims. While we need to honor conscience and the personal dignity of each human being as a moral agent, we need also to have a way of facing the realities of moral wrongdoing. And if there are realities of moral wrong, there are also realities of moral right—all of them grounded in, yet not reducible to, the agents of moral action.[6]

Fourth Challenge: All Morality Is Culturally Relative

Like subjectivism, *cultural relativism* points to something real that lies behind moral judgments. Where, for subjectivism, it was the interior conviction of the moral agent, for cultural relativism it is the society within which the moral agent has her identity. (For this argument, recognizing that societies have cultures and that cultures are found in societies, I will use the terms as rough equivalents.) According to cultural relativism, cultures and their societies are real and provide the standards of morality. So a cultural relativist could quite consistently say, of various individuals' actions, that they acted rightly or wrongly, as the case may be. She may pass judgment upon individuals and upon particular acts, and indeed upon groups and characteristic behaviors. What she may not do is to say that these judgments of right and wrong have any standing that goes beyond the culture within which she stands.

The plausibility of this view derives most deeply, I believe, from the fact that none of us started out independent of all societies. Human beings have parents (even if they don't know their parents); they have societies in which they are reared (even if their societies are dysfunctional); they must be educated because, as a result of evolution, post-natal education in humans has superseded much that in other animals is had by instinct. These indications are what we mean when we say that human beings are social animals. While it is true that we can make and re-make societies, the more basic truth is that we are the products of societies. Before individuals can make societies, societies will have had to make those individuals.

Our indebtedness to the societies that brought us into being and nurtured us to maturity encompasses much more than that of which we can be consciously aware. When we think reflectively about moral questions, we will realize that our moral views and convictions have been profoundly shaped by our parents, our teachers, and our companions.

And yet that realization can come to us with a jolt—and in that jolt can be found a recognition of the limits of relativism. A white American born in the second half of the twentieth century, for instance, might become aware—through a chance remark of one of his teachers—that he has been educated in ways that are racially prejudiced. He becomes aware that he has been unfathomably conditioned by his culture, while simultaneously he acquires a critical distance on that very conditioning. I remember as a child hearing an adult I trusted tell me that blacks (that's not the word she used) and whites shouldn't marry. "It's not fair to the children" was her reason. Alarm bells went off in my mind as I realized that I could harbor unknown racist attitudes—and that at the same time I could critique and reject them. Yet that adult with her uncritical attitude was correct to this extent: in certain cultural contexts indeed a biracial child would be ostracized.

So cultural relativism is onto something. We do acquire moral judgments from our cultures. And it is also quite plainly true that various cultures have made varying judgments about moral matters. Racial intermarriage is verboten in some cultures. I mentioned earlier that polygamy and collecting interest on money are practices that have sometimes been approved and, in other cultures, sometimes judged to be wrong. Cultures, that is to say, influence our moral judgments, but from one culture to another there seems to be no consistency of moral judgment. Therefore, on this view, it is impossible for us to discuss morality except from within our given culture—and that means that any moral claims we end up making are *nothing more than* the views of "our" culture.

To answer cultural relativism, all it would take would be for you to discover one point on which you think a cultural practice is simply wrong, wrong without qualification. I left the case of that biracial child hanging a couple of paragraphs ago. I hope it bothered you. If it is wrong to ostracize a child on account of his parentage, then any culture that would do so is, to that extent, morally at fault. Please note what we have done: we have passed judgment upon a culture. And our claim is not that, according to "our" culture, such an action is wrong; and we are certainly not saying that "our" culture is better than the other culture. We are making instead the supervening claim that *that action is wrong no matter what the culture is.*

Perhaps you disagree with me about biracial children. Then is there anything that you judge to be wrong regardless of the context? If a culture tolerated forcible sexual intercourse—rape— would you then say that rape is a matter of moral indifference in that culture? Or would you want to say something like, "It is wrong that they tolerate this inhuman practice"?

Such are the stakes. There are difficult questions here of how, on the one hand, to identify elements of cultural practices and moral judgments that are particular to given societies at given times and places, and on the other, to identify elements of practices and judgments that are universal and apply to all humans everywhere. But we do not have to be able to sort out such matters with complete certainty in order to reject the challenge of cultural relativism. All we need to do is to affirm that there is at least one thing concerning which we are willing to say it is always and everywhere wrong. If there is so much as one such thing, then we are affirming that morality stands higher than culture. And although it may be difficult to grasp a morality that is above societies and cultures (since we humans ineluctably arise within societies and live within various cultures), nonetheless we will refuse to deny morality's existence as a source of judgment upon societies and cultures.

In this last argument, the reader may have sensed an incipient claim that there is something about being a human that lies behind moral judgments. In an offhand phrase, I referred to tolerance of rape as an "inhuman" practice. Most things that people would propose as possible candidates for the category "always and every-where wrong" are things that we would describe as "inhuman": child molestation, human sacrifice, genocide, and the like. This is the flip side of an important positive point to which we will return: ethics is about what makes a good human being.

Christian Ethics, like All Theology, Defends Reason

To see the reasonableness of discourse about ethical matters—to see, that is, that it is not unreasonable to try to persuade one another and to try to understand what is truly right and good for human beings—is to see something very much in accord with Christian theology (and thus Christian ethics). And that is because Christianity is a faith that defends reason.

A potential Christian might wonder: if I join this religion, do I leave my brain behind? Some detractors charge that Christians aren't allowed to think for themselves and instead have to follow what the Bible says or what the church or some other authority figure tells them. Roman Catholics may be caricatured as mindless puppets of the pope, and evangelical Protestants as folks required to read the Bible credulously and unthinkingly. Yet the charge could be made against any Christian: to have faith—it is asserted—is to reject reason, because faith and reason are opposites. Is this correct?

To the contrary, Christians, through careful pondering, have long realized that faith and reason must fit together. Theology has, as one of its perennial tasks, the upholding and defense of reason. The opening words of St. John's Gospel are, as it were, "Exhibit A" in the theological case for reason. Those famous words are: "In the beginning was the Word." The Greek that's here translated "Word" is *logos*, a term that's obviously cognate to "logic" but possesses a broad meaning that encompasses "word," "speech," "narration," and "expression." For the pre-Christian Greek philosophers Plato and Aristotle, *logos* was a "rational explanation." Philo of Alexandria, the Jewish philosopher from the time of Christ, taught that *logos* was the reason in the mind of God, which was also the rational structure of nature and morality.[7]

So at the beginning of St. John's Gospel, the author points us to "the beginning," and there, he says, "was the Word." Christianity asserts that something reasonable is at the beginning of all things. The universe, that is to say, makes sense. It is intelligible.

This is a remarkable claim. It means that the rational mind is congruent with reality. It means that scientific investigation is possible, for the way things are (as products of a creative intelligence) can be truly investigated and potentially understood by us (as intelligent beings). Built into the meaning of rationality is inter-communicability: if you and I are both rational beings, we will be able to communicate with one another. And if the universe we live in is itself rational, if at its "beginning" lies some great being whose very name bespeaks reason, then we might well be able to understand the universe, to discover its laws and principles, and come to conscious awareness of our place within it.

An example of this is given by Augustine of Hippo (A.D. 354–430) in his *Confessions*. As a man in his 20s, Augustine was deeply involved with the Manichean religion. But he became troubled when he found in its writings an account of eclipses and other such astronomical events that was incompatible with the account given by (as we would say) science. When Augustine realized that even the high officials of the Manichees could not give an explanation that would reconcile their scriptures with science, he began the process of disassociating himself from their religion. A key reason why Augustine was able, eventually, to accept Christianity was because he learned that in Christianity faith and reason were not opposed to each other.[8]

It can appear a puzzling thing. The affirmation of reason is *a claim made by faith*. It is faith which says, "In the beginning was the Word." It is faith that tells us reason is at the heart of things. So we are presented with a dialectic of faith and reason. How does the dialectic function?

We could start with reason. It provides us with some things that we can see are true. But faith grants the one who has it claims about other things that faith claims are true also. These truths claimed by faith are not things that can be proven by reason. But a person of faith then strives to grasp, as best she can, the reasonableness of the truths given by faith. In particular, she will endeavor to show that the truths of faith are *not contrary to reason*. For instance, that God exists is a truth that can be known by reason simply reflecting on the world that we are given. (I am not giving the argument but just stating the conclusion.[9]) If we grant that as true (and I think there are good reasons to do so), it does not follow that we know anything about what God is. In particular, it would not follow that we know that God is the Trinity as professed by Christians. So God's existence as the creative cause of all things is a truth of reason, but God's being as Trinity is a truth of faith. Yet a person of faith cannot stop here. She must also inquire as to whether the claim about the Trinity is irrational. In particular, she will want to have rebuttals for any particular arguments purporting to show that the Trinity is irrational. Christian theologians have attempted to do just that: to show that claims of the irrationality of faith do not stand up. If they didn't care to do so—if, that is, Christian theologians were content to leave faith and reason as irreconcilable matters—then they would have failed to be true to a basic claim of Christianity!

Thus theology has as a part of its task the necessity of defending reason. This task of theology is thought by many cultural critics today to be of particular moment. For late-modern Western culture is no longer intolerant of belief *per se*; to the contrary, it seems to be happy to believe many things without care for their rationality or coherence. Such thinking divides the human person into various parts, and then fails to put the person back together with integrity. By defending reason against such dehumanizing forces, Christianity defends the integrity of the human person, and thus the congruence of faith and reason and, with it, the comprehensibility of the person and of the world.

Hence, Christian faith does not begin with the abandonment of reason, but with the opposite: it begins with the affirmation of reason. It is a fundamental Christian affirmation to say that reason is key to the universe.

Pope Benedict XVI in his pre-papal theological career captured well this tension and complementarity. He wrote that theology is based on two dialectically-related claims. "1) In Christian faith reason comes to light; faith precisely as faith wants reason. 2) Through Christian faith reason comes to light; reason presupposes faith as its environment."[10] The complementarity of reason and faith to the benefit of each was also the theme of his lecture, as pope, at the University of Regensburg in 2006. In this lecture Benedict develops the meaning of the opening of St. John's Gospel.

Is the conviction that acting unreasonably contradicts God's nature merely a Greek idea, or is it always and intrinsically true? I believe that here we can see the profound harmony between what is Greek in the best sense of the word and the biblical understanding of faith in God. Modifying the first verse of the Book of Genesis, the first verse of the whole Bible, John began the prologue of his Gospel with the words: "In the beginning was the *logos*." ... *Logos* means both reason and word—a reason which is creative and capable of self-communication, precisely as reason. John thus spoke the final word on the biblical concept of God, and in this word all the often toilsome and tortuous threads of biblical faith find their culmination and synthesis.[11]

In recent times, church leaders have seen the need, not to argue for the compatibility of faith and reason, but for the humane importance of reason itself. In this Benedict continues a trajectory found in the thought of his predecessor John Paul II, both as pope and earlier as priest and bishop in Poland, who employed the defense of reason as part of his defense of the human person.[12] His 1998 encyclical on the subject, *Fides et ratio*, has been rightly interpreted as an effort to restore faith in reason.

How then does the defense of reason apply to Christian ethics? As a work of theology, Christian ethics will include a defense of what reason can show us about moral matters. And Christian ethics will not understand itself as being opposed to reason. What this chapter has done by defending the reasonableness of talk about moral matters is a work of theology, a work, that is, of Christian ethics. The next chapter will look more closely at what is Christian about Christian ethics. But we can already identify a few things that we will not expect to find. We will not expect Christian ethics to be God telling people to do things that don't make sense. We will not expect Christian ethics to be separated, as by a chasm, from reason. Christian ethics may turn out to be more than reason would expect, but it will not turn out to be unreasonable.

*   *   *

Notes for Further Reading

In the arrangement of these four challenges to the reasonableness of ethics, I have followed in general the organization given the subject in Part One of Alban McCoy's *An Intelligent Person's Guide to Christian Ethics* (London: Continuum, 2004). McCoy's interpretation of some points, however, differs from that presented here. I have used his book with introductory theology classes, where the student feedback has been positive.

For a straightforward philosophical classic on the weaknesses of amoralism, subjectivism, and relativism, see Bernard Williams, *Morality: An Introduction to Ethics* (New York: Harper & Row, 1972; repr. as Canto edn, Cambridge: Cambridge University Press, 1993). Williams shows the illogic of the amoralist position, for instance, by showing that it is essentially, and necessarily, parasitical on some existing moralism. (Williams, I should note, thinks that any religious talk is "incurably unintelligible" [p. 72], and thus his arguments against amoralism, subjectivism, and relativism cannot be suspected of religious motivation.)

Also useful is Robert Spaemann, *Basic Moral Concepts* (trans. T. J. Armstrong; London: Routledge, 1989), a concise philosophical treatment of basic ethical questions (good, evil, pleasure, self-interest, conscience, and so forth). The translator provides a bibliography of works in English that both support and oppose the views taken by Spaemann, so that a student may use it to go further into the philosophical issues on any particular concept of interest.

For a guide to the primary texts in ethics, principally philosophical and Western, but also including some Eastern and religious texts, see David E. Cooper ed. *Ethics: The Classic Readings* (Oxford: Blackwell, 1998). Cooper here gives us 17 substantial excerpts of about 15 pages each from Plato to Stevenson, including Eastern writers such as Mencius. He also includes Aquinas, Butler, and Kierkegaard. With his introductions, the breadth of this work serves well for college students and teachers alike.

Papal encyclicals can be found on the Vatican's website, www. vatican.va. The reader may wish to take a look at John Paul II's 1998 encyclical *Fides et Ratio* (mentioned above in this chapter), in which John Paul develops some of his characteristic personalist themes: the relationship of faith and reason, the necessity of both, and the church's concern for the whole human being. For the Latin text, a new English translation, and thoughtful ecumenical commentary, see Laurence Paul Hemming and Susan Frank Parsons (eds), *Restoring Faith in Reason: A New Translation of the Encyclical Letter* Faith and Reason *of Pope John Paul II Together with a Commentary and Discussion* (London: SCM Press, 2002).

CHAPTER TWO

What's Christian about Christian Ethics?

Why Christian ethics is not just for Christians, not just doing what the Bible says, not just entering the Christian narrative or community—but living as fully human

Different Meanings of "Christian Ethics"

What is the work of the adjective when we say "Christian ethics"? It seems natural enough to use the term, "Christian ethics," yet reflection brings perplexity. When we say "Christian ethics" do we mean the ethics that pertains to Christians—and indeed, perhaps to Christians only? That is, are there different ethics for different religions? (In the U.S., there is not only a learned society in Christian ethics, but there are also, for instance, the Society of Jewish Ethics and the Society for the Study of Muslim Ethics. Are such societies studying the systems of ethics that pertain to members of their various faiths?) Or—a second possibility—when we say "Christian ethics" do we mean there is an ethics that applies to the "religious realm" as distinct from the rest of life (thus taking "Christian ethics" as a specialized term in parallel with "business ethics," "bioethics," and so forth)? Or—a third alternative—is that word "Christian" just an empty shell, a hollowed-out relic of the past, an adjective that we might use more or less synonymously with "decent"? In this sense, "a Christian woman" would mean (only) a woman who is strong or kind or thoughtful (whatever it is we think of when we say "decent"), and "a Christian action" would simply be a good action, and so forth.

As I set out these alternatives, none of them seems adequate to me. The first, that "Christian ethics" is the ethics that applies to Christians only, has perhaps the strongest appeal. If one adopts or participates in a particular faith, then it seems natural to suppose that the content of that faith would shape one's life, and thus that there would be an ethics to correspond to that faith. It would follow that if one were a Christian, then there should be manifestations of Christianity in one's life, an ethos that is visible and describable. So far, so clear. Yet ethical claims, at least normally, are claims about what it is right and wrong to do, claims to describe actions or patterns of behavior or acquired dispositions (virtues and vices) as good or bad, indeed, good or evil. These are claims not limited to a particular religion. To take a very simple example, it seems to fall short of what we mean by ethics to say, "For me as a Christian, kicking a street-person as I walk past him is wrong, but if you aren't a Christian, it might or might not be wrong, depending on your beliefs." Kicking a sprawling man on the sidewalk as you walk past is either wrong or not—it is hard to see how its wrongness could be dependent on your Christian faith or lack of it. (Which is not to say either that you could act in ignorance of something being wrong, or that in some circumstances something may be wrong that in other circumstances would be permitted or required. If a runaway food-cart is careening down the sidewalk, you might be compelled to move the man forcibly and peremptorily in order to get him out of harm's way.)

The second alternative was to take "Christian ethics" as somehow analogous to "business ethics" and the like: namely, an ethics that applies to a particular realm. This view, too, has something to say for itself. "Business ethics," for instance, takes common and universal ethical notions and applies them to the world of business. It is in large part a specification of more universal notions to the particular activities of business. Thus, the notion of truth-telling, which (let us stipulate) is an important notion to ethics, needs to be applied to sales practices, advertising, investor relations, and the like. A corporation will cultivate its own ethos that will be instantiated in explicit policies and procedures that specify what truth-telling requires in various circumstances. We could then judge a corporation as achieving a certain ethical excellence through its cultivation of an ethos of truth-telling. And we could judge particular persons or departments within a corporation as succeeding or falling short according to how well they instantiated the ethos, policies, and procedures governing truth-telling.

But in this sense, as the application of broader notions of ethics to a particular realm, "Christian ethics," it seems to me, would have to refer to the practices and procedures of Christian bodies: churches, seminaries, hospitals, schools, and other Christian organizations. One would think, then, of such things as documents that set forth expectations of sexual conduct, and definitions and descriptions of sexual misconduct. One would think, carrying this forward, of policies and procedures that Christian bodies would follow when their officers or leaders (ordained and non-ordained), employees, and perhaps members at large, are accused or suspected of sexual misconduct. These matters are important, as no one can deny after the scandals (which are hardly exclusively Roman Catholic) of recent decades. But is this what we normally mean by "Christian ethics," the ethics of one kind of institution (a religious institution) among all the other institutions of society? I doubt that one reader in a hundred picked up this Guide expecting to find guidance on how to run the institution of a church. (Not that Christian ethics has nothing to say about Christian institutions! It's just that we normally expect it to be covering a broader field, not to be so specialized.)

The third alternative, that "Christian ethics" means simply "the ethics that any decent person will be following," also has something in its favor, if not much. When, a century ago, the Christian ecumenical movement was getting underway, one influential strand of thought believed that separated Christian bodies could unite in Christian action for the good of the world, even if they could not overcome their doctrinal divisions. It became a slogan: "Doctrine divides, service unites." Behind this slogan was a naive optimism that everyone would agree on the content of Christian ethics. In reality, such agreement as there was on ethics survived only as the unexamined deposit from past Christian centuries. As the doctrines of Christianity came less and less to be accepted by society, then (after an understandable lag of a couple of generations) the corresponding ethics of Christianity also came into question. This questioning goes on within the churches today, and sometimes it is quite strident—to the point that, today, the voices urging concord have turned the old slogan on its head. Today the voices urging concord say, "Since we agree on basic doctrines like the Trinity and the Incarnation, can't we just get along even though we disagree on ethics?" The slogan today would be, "Ethics divides, doctrine unites."

So it is naive (and shows ignorance of history) to think that, although the doctrinal content of "Christian" may be disputed, we can ignore that doctrine and focus on a presumed agreement on the moral content of the term "Christian." I will argue theologically (and this entire Guide is, in effect, such an argument) that Christian doctrine and Christian ethics are inseparable. However, one fundamental aspect of Christian doctrine is its expressed catholicity. Keep in mind that the word "catholic" is a noble word denoting "universality." (On a mundane level, a person who appreciates the fine cuisine of many cultures could properly be described as having catholic tastes.) Christian claims are put forth as "catholic" claims, as claims about the whole truth that is for every human being, past, present, and future. Christian doctrine is, in every sense, catholic doctrine. And so Christian ethics, I say, must be ethics for all people. Christian ethics, that is (if I am correct), turns out in fact to be the ethics that is followed by good human beings.

Christian Ethics and the Bible

But there is more to be said about the first alternative: that "Christian ethics" refers to the ethics that applies to Christian people. I claimed above that this alternative seems to run afoul of our sense that declarations of wrongness are not dependent on the beliefs of those who are acting. Whether it is wrong for you to kick a man on the sidewalk cannot hang on the beliefs you espouse (although it may well hang on your judgment of the facts and the context of the particular situation).

Yet if we dig a little deeper, some questions may disturb this conclusion. Think, for starters, about the situation I put forth as an example: you are walking down a sidewalk, and there is a person sprawled along the side of it. Just in those few words, I have had to *tell a story*, however sparely done, about the situation. I laid out a scene for you, I put "you" into it, and I set the scene in motion, as it were, as I identified an action that you might do (although I hope you would never do it): kick the man as you passed by.

Now this is starting to take on interest. We have two characters that we have identified in the scene: the one on the sidewalk, and the one walking by. And what does it mean to be a "character"? If the story (or the example) isn't very good, then a character is just a "stick figure," a "placeholder," something "shallow" that in the end is not very interesting. But if the story (or example) is a good one, the characters in it will have "depth" and "texture" and "complexity." And what does it mean for them to have such deep, textured, or complex characters? It means we can tell interesting stories about them. Let me put it this way: interesting characters are part of interesting stories. They are characters in significant narratives.

What would it take to make my simple illustration more interesting, which is to say, to make the two characters in it more textured and complex? First, with regard to the man on the sidewalk, we would want to know *why* he is sprawled out there. What has happened to him? Is he the victim of an injustice (a mugging, perhaps, or a wrongful eviction)? Or does he have a history of substance addiction? Or has he freely chosen to take up this bit of public real estate? He could be there voluntarily, or he could be a person who has lost control of his will—and so forth. There could be many different reasons for his presence on the sidewalk. And each reason is nothing more than *a narrative account of who he is*. To answer the question "Who is this person?" is always to narrate some sort of biography.

The other character is "you." Who are "you" as you walk past this man? You may be a student, late to your ethics class with the frustratingly punctual Professor Austin, with not a moment to lose on account of any interruption of your plans. Or you may be a police officer, or a judge, or a clerk, or a priest. Does it matter? Of course it matters: who you are (and what's going on with you at that moment) will affect whether and how you "see" this man on the sidewalk. And what is your own story? What is your history of encounters with other street people? Have you ever befriended a stranger, or been harmed by one? What story do you bring to this encounter?

Note what has happened. We started with a simple example of everyday urban life—walking past a person on the sidewalk—but it has turned into an event of the confluence of two personal narratives. To understand what we do, we look to who we are; to understand who we are, we look to biography. Actions come from characters; characters are found in narratives. Narrative is inescapable.

Now let us suppose that "you," the person who is approaching this sprawled human being, are a Christian. This means that, along the way of your life, your understanding of things has been shaped by your Christianity. It happens, of course, to various degrees, and you might or might not have a clear understanding of things Christian. But to one degree or another, as you approach the man on the sidewalk, you bring with you a version of the *Christian narrative*. Your own narrative, as it were, includes or carries the Christian narrative. What is contained in the narrative that Christians tell? A first answer would be the contents of the Bible. And central to the Bible are the gospels (Matthew, Mark, Luke, and John) that tell of the life and teachings (and death and resurrection) of Jesus. To some extent, you will be carrying that. And you might even be aware of one particular story that Jesus told (according to St. Luke). A man was on a road between two cities, where he was set upon by robbers, beaten up, and abandoned. Several distinguished citizens (including a priest) walked past him and did nothing. But one man stopped, washed his wounds, brought him to the innkeeper of the next village, and paid for his food and lodging until he was better. Jesus ends that story with a question: who proved himself a neighbor to the man on the road?

The answer, of course, is the one who helped him. And the question of "neighbor" resonates broadly. This story, significantly, falls within a broader biblical narrative in which it is taught that we should love our neighbor as ourselves.[1]

What does this mean for "you," a Christian walking past this sprawled character on the sidewalk? It means that your response is shaped, positively or negatively, by the Christian story of which you are a part. To put it another way, it means that what you do can be explained (at least in part) by reference to the Christian narrative that has shaped your character.

Now this is not an easy thing. Just because Jesus told the story of the good Samaritan doesn't mean that any of us should stop and help any particular person we pass on the sidewalk. But it does mean that every one of us (if we are a Christian) will be shaped by the question of "proving ourselves" to be "a neighbor" and thus "loving our neighbor as ourselves." It seems to me that often the Christian story doesn't so much tell us what to do as it *tells us the questions that our lives should be answers to.* So the Christian story doesn't tell me *how* to love my neighbor, or even who my neighbor is; it causes me to ask, "How am I proving myself neighbor?" Christians thus will seek to discover what it means to love a neighbor in a concrete situation. A Christian's autobiography will be, in part, a narrative answer to such questions embedded in the broader Christian narrative.

There is much more to it than this. There is, for instance, the matter of falling short and failing to do what one should have done. This too is part of the Christian narrative: the business of "coming to yourself"[2] and repenting of having done wrong and being turned around. So, in this example, it's not only what "you" do as you pass by, but how, later, you reflect upon it and perhaps repent. And another element, besides recollection and repentance, is the implicit requirement of creativity. A magnificent feature of Jesus' commandment to love our neighbor as ourselves is that it is a commandment we can never be finished with. We may have done some very good and loving things today. But tomorrow will call for new decisions in fresh circumstances. One is never finished with "proving" that one is a neighbor, that is, with making oneself into a neighbor.

To summarize: *a Christian is a person who carries within herself some version of the Christian narrative.* And therefore: *in giving an account of the actions of a Christian, it will make sense to turn to the Christian narrative.*

The author should come clean here. I live in New York City. Every day of my life I walk past at least a few people who are sprawled on the street. With rare exceptions, I do not stop to try to help them. I do make an effort to look at them, and if they look at me, I try to register that I am seeing them. If asked for money, I decline and say "I can't." But I do not kick them. So I am not able, or at least I do not, demonstrate positive love for them. But on the other hand I do not, by positive action, deny that they are my neighbor, by giving them the shove that I would give to a piece of trash in the way. I may not be a very good Christian, but still it seems to me that I can account for these decisions and actions of mine on the basis of the Christian narrative, which is shaping me nonetheless (still).

Narrative and Community

If "Christian ethics" means the ethics that pertains to Christians (our first initial alternative), then the preceding discussion shows that such ethics points to narratives that are carried by characters who somehow themselves carry a version of the Christian narrative. But is narrative indeed such a fundamental concept?

For one might object that all I did in the past section was to show that Christians have a *concept* of "neighbor." Admittedly, it is a concept that comes from their special Christian narrative as given in the Bible. But in the end all Christian talk of "neighbor" amounts to the same thing as our secular or non-Christian notion of "humanity" or "human being." Indeed, no decent person would kick a man who is down, because even when down that man is a fellow human being. Christians just use the concept of "neighbor" to express this same point that everyone (or, at least, every decent person) would admit.

But there is more to the point that is being made about narratives. As I've noted, narratives include characters, and rich, textured, interesting characters are found in good narratives. Let me push this further. I think we can say that each of us humans is made who we are by the narratives that we live by.

Consider me, a sort of intellectual priest who fumblingly tries to live in a way that's true and faithful as a Christian. This means that I try to live by the Christian story. And so I'm troubled, perhaps convicted of sin, when I realize that something about my life falls short of or doesn't fit with that story. I try to live a life that is shaped by that story. There are of course other stories, other narratives, that shape the story of my life. An important question is whether those other stories are compatible with the Christian narrative, and whether the Christian narrative is the predominant narrative within which I live.

When we consider these various narratives, it is important to take in how it is they come to any of us. *We receive a narrative by being part of a community*. There are, in fact, no narratives without communities. Communities are groups of people who receive, shape, and pass on narratives.

How then can we evaluate the truth of a narrative? This is the stickiest point of "narrative theology" or "narrative ethics." For if narrative is fundamental, then there is no way to get outside narratives, no external and objective vantage point from which one could stand in judgment above and over competing narratives. A character *in* a story cannot rise up in judgment *over* that story.

To judge a story, then, the only criteria one has are such things as richness, texture, and interestingness. To say it again, a good narrative is one that has and produces interesting characters. Stanley Hauerwas, the American ethicist whose decades-long project has been to explore such matters, says that "[t]he ability to provide an adequate account of our existence is the primary test of the truthfulness of a social ethic."[3] The way to tell that a narrative (an "account of our existence") is true is to see if it is "adequate" (interesting, non-superficial, and so forth).

This I think is correct. Yet, unfortunately, such tests work best negatively, and they cannot be infallible. That is, it may well be possible, and perhaps even easy, to get agreement that a given social ethic *fails* adequately to account for our existence. The social ethic of the Ku Klux Klan is surely inadequate, as is any ethic that denies our fundamental conviction that all human beings are to be treated with dignity and respect. So we can rule out those narratives that we can see clearly fall short. But in such cases, the narratives that fall short are not ones that produce interesting characters. The test will not help us in those cases when we have competing rich narratives that each produce communities of characters who judge their own narrative to provide an adequate account of their existence.

And let us note that in the last paragraph I have done something that should seem a bit of a cheat. I have made a point by using as an example of an ethic that of the Klan, which ethic is widely despised. I believe, as I'm sure my readers do, that this ethic is rightly despised. But that's because I believe, as I also assume my readers do, that there is something about every human being that makes her worthy of respect. We would probably say that every human being has "dignity," and we might speak of the "sanctity" of human beings. But when we use such language, are we speaking of *qualities* that *inhere* in individual human beings—qualities, that is, which individual human beings have *quite apart from any narrative that they live by*, and thus *quite apart from any community within which they come to be*? To make such a supposition *within* narrative ethics would indeed be a "cheat," because our premise in this argument here has been that there are no such narrative-free qualities, just as there are no narrative-free human beings and there are no community-free individuals. The narrative conception of human being is that we are characters within narratives and that we receive our narratives from our various communities. If this is radically true, then we may not try to justify the truth or adequacy of our narratives by reference to non-narrative notions. "Dignity" and "sanctity" and all other such notions must themselves be given by narratives: they cannot provide a foothold for a judgment that rises above and over competing narratives.

All that having been said about the impossibility of judging between various narratives, narrative ethics may still be true. That is, it may still be the case that we are constituted as the characters we are by the narratives according to which we live—narratives that come to us by means of communities that are themselves shaped by those narratives even as they transmit them and shape them historically. Christian ethics, then, would consist in *trying to live by the Christian narrative*, a narrative that *shapes the Christian community which itself, in transmitting the narrative and incorporating new persons within it, also shapes the narrative through history.*

There Are Rules in the Bible, but the Bible Is More than Rules

If we describe Christian ethics as "trying to live by the Christian narrative," what we are really talking about is trying to live by the Bible. The Christian narrative is given to us by the Bible; it is in the Bible that we find the Christian narrative. But Christian narrative ethics takes a particular approach to the Bible.

For Christian narrative ethics, the Bible is not a rule-book. Clearly the Bible contains rules. There are, famously, ten commandments (Exod. 20.2-17; Deut. 5.6-21). And many more than ten: a lot of the Old Testament bubbles over with commands. "Your lamb shall be without blemish," for instance, is part of the preparation for the ritual Passover meal (Exod. 12.5). There are laws for family, for society, for agriculture, for the treatment of animals, for food, and so forth (examples abound throughout the Pentateuch—Genesis through Deuteronomy—and lie behind many verses in Proverbs, and stories such as Ruth are built upon them). The New Testament, too, has a good number of commands. In the letters attributed to St. Paul, which take up about half of the New Testament, the apostle issues instructions for—among many other things—how to celebrate the Eucharist (1 Cor. 11.17-32), how to organize the home (Eph. 6.1-9), and to pray for rulers and respect their rightful authority (1 Tim. 2.1-2; cf. Rom. 13.1-8). And even Jesus himself, in the gospels that constitute the core of the New Testament, gave many commands, among them: to baptize and teach (Mt. 28.19-20), to love God and neighbor (Mk 12.29-31 and parallels), to break bread for his remembrance (Lk. 22.19), not to hold unjustified anger (Mt. 5.22; cf. Lk. 15.25-32), not to prize self-preservation (Mk 8.34-37 and parallels). So it is undeniable that rules, commands, and laws run throughout the Bible.

But for all that the Bible is wrongly thought of as a rule-book. And the reason is that the Bible contains so much more than just rules. It is in fact a great story, and Christian narrative ethics is the attempt to grasp and indwell the Bible as a whole, as one comprehensive story that runs from the beginning of the world to its end. Each of the rules I mentioned in the last paragraph is found as part of this story, some of them at very particular moments (such as "Do this in remembrance of me"), others as recurrent themes (such as "Love your neighbor as yourself").

As a great story, the Bible *has characters* and can *produce characters* (and perhaps more to the point: it can produce *character*). For the people who read the Bible, its characters populate the mind and the world (the interior and the exterior landscapes). There are Adam and Eve, Cain and Abel, Abraham and Sarah, Ishmael and Isaac, Esau and Jacob, Tamar and Judah—just to take a few of the characters of the first book, Genesis. There are also characters in the stories told by the characters in the Bible: like the poor man with his single beloved ewe lamb, in the parable told by Nathan to David (2 Sam. 12), or the already-mentioned traveler who, beaten and robbed and abandoned, was later assisted by the Samaritan, in the parable told by Jesus. It is a rich and complex world, the biblical narrative, rich and complex precisely because it *has characters*. And those biblical characters tend to *produce characters*, the people perhaps like you and me who have come to know these stories and find these stories affecting our lives.

Seen as a great narrative, the Bible produces *character* in its effect upon us, making us into the people we are. This happens not so much because we take on the rules we find in the Bible—for just taking on rules is an exterior thing, it doesn't really shape us—but because we *enter the world of the Bible* or, perhaps better, *the world of the Bible enters into our world* and we start living as characters in a double-narrative, the narrative written in the Bible and the narrative being written as we live our own lives.

That, in short, is the principal point about narrative ethics: rather than a matter of obeying commandments, ethics is the effort to shape our lives as we endeavor to live according to the story that we purport to live by. This happens on various levels at once—not only in concrete choices, but in habits and qualities of character that are formed over time.

Critique of Both Narratives and Rules

We could summarize our argument so far in the following way. The most likely place to look for the content or meaning of "Christian ethics" would seem to be the Bible. But what do we seek to find in the Bible? On the one hand, it might be distinctive commands or rules that Christians desire to live by: the Ten Commandments, the Sermon on the Mount, and so forth. These rules might be explicitly given in the Bible, or they might be more subtly discerned—a principle of nonviolence, say, or an "ethic of love." But any summary articulation of biblical commands or rules runs up against the problem that the Bible is so much more than that summary articulation.

Hence the turn to narrative ethics, the effort to understand Christian ethics as a "living into" the biblical narrative. In this approach, Christian ethics is a way of life that strives to locate the narrative of one's own life (which is not the life of an individual only, but of individuals in Christian community) in significant relationship to the scriptural narrative. This is a promising approach, in that it deals with the textual character of

Scripture (and reckons with the ongoing need for improvisation as one "reads" one's life). It also has interesting theological promise, in that, as creatures of God whose existence is at every moment the gift of the creator, we are rather like characters in a lengthy, on-going story whose author has made us real, complex, and interesting.

Yet whenever an attempt is made to specify what makes *Christian* narrative ethics distinctive, the only acceptable answer is that it is *that* narrative ethics which takes the Bible as the serious and meaningful narrative into which we are to live. If one presses for something more specific, some elucidation of what makes the Bible distinctive, or some description of how Christian narrative ethics differs from other sorts of ethics, it turns out that there is nothing to say. For if one were to articulate some principles or themes that are purported to be distinctive to Christian narrative ethics, one would by that very articulation have simplified and flattened out the biblical narrative. Christian narrative ethics is no more captured in a description of it as a search for a "peaceable kingdom" or the continual attempt to prove oneself a neighbor— however central those themes are—than it is captured in a set of laws or commands.

It is possible, in fact, simply to change any theme into a command. So, for example, if the narrative theme of Christian ethics is asserted to be "the search, the longing for, and the striving to live into God's peaceable kingdom," the corresponding rule or command is: "We should above all else both individually and as Christian communities seek and long for and strive to live into God's peaceable kingdom." Or, to take an alternate example, if the narrative theme of Christian ethics is asserted to be "the ongoing prayerful search to prove myself and ourselves as neighbor," then the corresponding command is just: "Seek persistently to prove yourself a neighbor both individually and as a church body."

So narrative ethics, in the end, falls short at just the point where Christian rule-ethics falls short. Any attempt to describe the quality or characteristics of Christian narrative ethics will necessarily step outside the narrative, and in doing so will make reference (impermissible reference, according to the terms of narrative ethics) to some standard outside the narrative.

"There's No Such Thing as Christian Ethics"

Yet the fact of the matter is that the Christian narrative itself points outside itself. It is, one could say, intrinsically self-transcending. Let me explain.

The broad scope of the Bible is a narrative that begins with God creating the world and ends with the world passing through final judgment at which time there appears a new heaven and a new earth (which is somehow the same, original creation, but transformed). Between the beginning and the end, Jesus Christ enters the narrative as God Incarnate, a human being who is also the unique Son of God, who brings about the redemption of the world. So God creates, God redeems, and God is the end of all things.

We may indeed think of God as the author of all things. Creation means the giving of existence to things (and holding them in existence). Creation is not the rearrangement of already existing things into a new pattern, but rather the granting of being to something that, otherwise, would not exist. So God does not create by using tools or intermediaries. In Genesis 1, we are told that God creates by speaking. "Authorship" is a perfectly acceptable way of talking about this.

Now the author of a story cannot be a character in a story. Even if the story is about the author, the author as such transcends what is said in the story. (All autobiographies fail to be complete; there is always more to the author than what he has told!) But a distinctive characteristic of the Christian narrative is that it claims the following: the Author of the world has entered into the world as a Character. In Jesus of Nazareth, the Author took on human nature and lived a complete human life, including death.

Thus, the Christian narrative claims to be self-transcending, to have within it a Character who, also, stands above and over the narrative. This Character, then, has the right and the capability to pass judgment over the narrative of the world. He can (and, it is claimed, will come again to do just this) judge all who are alive, all who have died, and all who will ever live. His judgment is redemptive, in that it allows the possibility for this narrative to become a true narrative: in him, the world can attain its purpose, can reach its fruition.

I picked up this way of speaking from the late and brilliantly creative theologian Herbert McCabe.[4] And if we accept *this* narrative, we are driven to make two further claims. First, that this narrative is the true narrative for the entire world, in particular for all human beings. It is the narrative over all other narratives. We will not be able to make an irrefutable argument for this conclusion (for we will always be characters within this narrative). Yet we will see that this claim is entailed by the narrative's own internal claim of self-transcendence.

Second, we will then say that, among the alternatives laid out at the beginning of this chapter, the third one turns out to be true in an unexpected way. "Christian ethics," that is to say, is just ethics for everybody.

Indeed, McCabe at one point says baldly: "there is no such thing as Christian ethics. There is just ethics."[5] Behind this provocative formulation is the christological claim that Jesus' entire identity is given by his obedience to his Father's command that he, Jesus, be fully human. Hence the Scriptures, understood properly as a grand narrative, are most fundamentally about the revelation of what it means to be human, a revelation finally given in the Incarnation, when the Son of God is sent by his Father to be—fully, completely—a human being. The Bible, that is, cannot speak directly about its Author; rather, it tells us about what it is to be human (including that its Author has become a human being).

McCabe also makes an anthropological claim. He says that what it means to be a human being—the human "essence" if you will—is to live in community with other humans, and that that community is most properly described as friendship. This fellowship is impossible to us, as we currently exist. We humans are divided against each other. (Indeed, we live by various and often competing narratives.) We will only be truly human when we are able to live in friendship with all others. It is in Christ that all people can (and ultimately, please God, will) live together. Jesus is fully human because he lives this way: in love for every person. Of course he was killed. But, living solely by love, his body would not remain in the grave.

Let me say more about the christological claim of Jesus' complete humanity. The classical Christian affirmation is that Jesus is at once fully human and fully divine; as a divine person who took on human nature, he is both man and God, without either of those mixing with or subtracting from the other.[6] This kind of talk seems contradictory, because, in the way we use nouns, nothing else can be at once and completely two different things. I can't be a man and a duck at one and the same time, for instance—although, if I were the product of some scheming, manipulative genetic researcher, I might be part-duck and part-man. Yet the claim about Jesus is not that he is part-man and part-God, but fully man and fully God.

But this seeming contradiction disappears when we realize that to be God is not to be any created thing. God, as the creator, is the source of other beings' existence; his existence cannot be caused by theirs. Thus God is no being in the universe. What this means is that we cannot place God alongside anything, even if only in our minds, and count them. God plus the universe do not make "two."[7] Hence, when we try to understand Jesus, we must purge our minds of any sense that we can put his divinity "alongside" his humanity. Jesus is not "humanity plus divinity." To be God, since it is not to be any countable thing, cannot be added onto anything else. Divinity is never a "plus factor." Whatever else it means for Jesus to be divine, it cannot mean that he "has" something that the rest of us do not have. Divinity is not a thing to be had.

So while we cannot understand what it means for Jesus to be divine—as the Bible cannot tell us how one of its characters is also its Author—we can realize that what we *see* in him is just sheer humanity. The fully divine human being, Jesus, in the remarkable formulation of the Roman Catholic Church's Second Vatican Council, "fully reveals man to man," showing us what it is to be human.[8] This christological claim then circles back to our anthropology.

Each of us humans is constituted by our relationships.[9] And to be fully human is to be constituted by relationships with all other human beings. We think wrongly when we consider a human being as an already-existing individual who then, as an act of will, decides to enter into societies of one sort or another. Although the picture of the sovereign individual is prevalent in Western culture, it prevails only by overlooking things like the development of a child and the use of language. Particularly the use of language points to the primacy of society for human beings, because meanings, concepts, and so forth are common property which we first share in before we, by our own contributions, shape and re-create. Societies create individuals, who arise out of societies and only then can critique and contribute to their societies' ongoing transformation and transmission.

But if to be human is to be constituted by one's relationships, all of us fall short of being fully human because we are constituted out of societies that are in some deep sense broken off from one another. Sometimes this is the basic matter of language: we simply don't understand one another. Sometimes it is a broader inability to understand: we have such different histories that we just don't know where the other society is coming from. And in addition there is the problem of sin, which distorts all relationships and corrupts some nearly completely: making the task of communication all the more difficult.

Sin—and evil generally—is understood by Christianity as being essentially a matter of falling short, of lacking something one ought to have. A sinful human being is, by virtue of her sin, less human than she would otherwise be. This falling short in our humanity is constitutional in that we are constituted by our relationships with other people. So when our societies are fractured, uncomprehending, separated, even hostile to one another, then our personal constitutions are diminished and our humanity suffers. The key point is the converse: *Jesus Christ, as the complete human being, is constituted by his relationship with all human beings.*

What is that relationship? It is "love" or "communication" or "availability" or "solidarity"—to pick just some of the words that have been used to characterize it. It is fundamentally that Jesus does not cut himself off from any person, but is in his being made by his love for all. We see in Jesus, in the striking formulation of McCabe's, two fundamental anthropological truths: To be human is to live by love. And to live by love, in the kind of world that we have brought about by our sin, is to be killed.[10]

Jesus, whose life achieved the finality of death, offers us something that comes not from his past but from his future. In his resurrection, Jesus brings the ultimate future of the human race into the present as a foretaste of our destiny in Christ. The brokenness of human beings, their failure to be fully human, will not be the last word. Death is followed by resurrection. In the end it will be possible to be human, to be constituted by relationship with all human beings. The risen Christ is the fully human being who succeeds in living by love with all human beings. To be in that Christ is our proffered destiny.

So: what Christianity teaches us about ethics has to do with what it means to be human. In that sense, in the end there is just human ethics.

The Fully Human Character Who Transcends the Narrative

Of the three alternatives for construing "Christian ethics" as laid out at the beginning of this chapter, it seemed most likely that Christian ethics would have to do with the ethics followed by Christian people. While such people will find quite a number of commandments in the Bible, the Bible nonetheless gives them something that goes beyond those commandments: a narrative that runs from the beginning of all things to their end, within which there are, besides commandments, several characters, accounts of what those characters have done, and a good number of shorter stories (sometimes told by one of the characters). This narrative, I have said, shapes the Christian community which bears it, and members of that community have had their own character formed through their efforts to live by that narrative.

If this were all that we could say, then we would be left with our initial problem of narrative relativism. Since our ethics would have been shaped by the Christian narrative, and since (as characters who are brought into being within narratives) we are unable to get outside our narratives, we would have to say that Christian ethics was *only* for those who lived in or by the Christian narrative. That is, whatever Christians might understand about the human good or human duties would pertain only to Christians. However, the specific Christian claim of the Incarnation is that the Author of all things has entered into the world as a Character. The claim of the Incarnation thus gives us "purchase" on the possibility of judging between narratives, and makes the claim that the Christian narrative is the narrative which encompasses and judges all other narratives. This, Christians in effect say, is true, even though it is impossible for any Christian (who remains a character in the story) to share the view of the Character in the story who is one in being with the Author.

The consequence for this Guide is the following. Thanks to its grounding in the fundamental Christian understandings of the Trinity and the Incarnation, Christian ethics turns out to be simply human ethics. That is to say, Christian ethics is not, in the end, about matters that pertain to some people (e.g., Christians) and not others. It is, rather, about being fully human.

Henceforth this Guide will take it as given that "Christian ethics" has as its subject matter the living of a fully human life. How then might we live more fully a human life? In the next chapter, I will explore three fundamental ways to give content to what it means to be fully human.

* * *

Notes for Further Reading

The student who wishes to study further the debate on the distinctiveness of Christian ethics would do well to read Joseph Fuchs, "Is There a Specifically Christian Morality?" in Charles E. Curran and Richard A. McCormick (eds), *The Distinctiveness of Christian Ethics* (Readings in Moral Theology No. 2; New York: Paulist Press, 1980), 3–19. In this article, which proved highly influential to post-Vatican II Roman Catholic moral theology, Fuchs makes a distinction, probably drawn from Immanuel Kant, between the "categorical" level and the "transcendental." The distinctiveness of Christian moral theology, he says, is in the "transcendental," a matter more of intentionality (attitudes and motivations) than of specific (categorical) content.

A brief and competent summary of the development of Roman Catholic moral theology in the second half of the twentieth century is found in Norbert Rigali, "New Horizons in Moral Theology," in *New Horizons in Theology* (ed. Terrence W. Tilley; College Theology Society Annual Volume 50; Maryknoll, N.Y.: Orbis, 2005), 40–55.

While widely followed, Fuchs has his critics. For a notable one, see Servais Pinckaers, *The Sources of Christian Ethics* (3rd edn; trans. Mary Thomas Noble; Washington, D.C.: Catholic University of America Press, 1995), 100–103. Students may appreciate

Pinckaers's more introductory treatment, *Morality, The Catholic View* (South Bend, Ind.: St. Augustine's Press, 2003), ch. 5.

Nigel Biggar has recently argued that Christians should seek integrity, not distinctiveness, in their moral theology—by which he means that Christian ethics should be of a piece with Christian theology in general and not excluding Christian worship and spiritual practices. It may turn out that, on particular matters (or rules or practices), Christian moral theology has slight difference from the ethics of a given secular society. In other words, there is no *a priori* reason for Christian ethics to be distinctive. Nonetheless, Christian ethics may often be in some tension with other ethics, for its motivation, and some of its content (according to Biggar), is distinctive. See his *Behaving in Public: How to Do Christian Ethics* (Grand Rapids, Mich.: Eerdmans, 2011), esp. ch. 1–2.

What might be examples of specifically Christian ethical content? Fuchs does seem to point to consecrated virginity as an example of an ethical matter on the categorical level that is distinctively Christian, and of Christian beliefs as providing motivation for moral action on the categorical level (Fuchs, 15–16). In this, Biggar follows him, and in doing so provides a telling example. We might well agree, he says, that there is a form of human flourishing that is given with our human nature, something that we could learn from reflection upon what we are. Such reflection could also lead us to grasp what dispositions and actions we need to have in order to achieve the goods that accord with our nature. We might agree, even, that all people have some capacity to grasp these goods and their requirements. *Nonetheless*, we have considerable disagreement in fact about what those goods are, "about whether, for example, communion with God is among them…. We [also] disagree about whether we may intentionally damage some goods for the sake of others—and if so, under what conditions" (Biggar, 35; cf. 41–2). Who is my equal? A fetus? An illegal immigrant? Despite the considerable disagreement among Christians on specific moral matters, Biggar holds that there is nonetheless specific Christian content to be had.

The conclusion argued for in the present chapter—that *Christian* ethics is about *human* flourishing and is thus *human* ethics—does not foreclose the possibility of specific Christian content to Christian ethics. For whatever insights and motivations may come from the Christian narrative, and may be formed in the persons and communities themselves formed by that narrative, they are in the end insights and motivations for an ethics that is for all human beings. Because the gospel is for everyone—because the Christian narrative is self-transcending and cosmically inclusive—the proper adjective for Christian ethics is "human."

CHAPTER THREE

Three Approaches to Being Fully Human

Namely: doing our duty, maximizing the good, and cultivating virtue

The Schema

If Christian ethics is about becoming fully human, what is the deep structure to that? According to one way of thinking, we fulfill our humanity by conforming ourselves to that which it is given to us to do. There are presented to us, according to this view, rules or laws that we are supposed to follow, and our human, moral fulfillment is found precisely in our willing obedience to those given commands. A second and strikingly different picture is that our fulfillment is found in bringing about an increase of the good in the world. If I can make the world a better place, then to that extent I have fulfilled myself as a moral being. Finally, a third view would try to combine these first two in a vision of flourishing that involves both rules and the good in the formation of human character.

Thus, schematically, there are three ways to approach ethics. The first emphasizes duty: ethics is a matter of doing what one ought to do, period. Alternately, one may emphasize the outcome: ethics is a matter of maximizing the human good (say, by bringing about the greatest good for the greatest number). In recent decades, and often out of the perceived interminability of debates between these two approaches, a third way has gained many adherents. It is to emphasize the excellent functioning of the human person: ethics is about the development of virtues.[1]

Each of these approaches can be put in Christian terms. One's duty may be understood as given by divine command, expressed perhaps through revealed law given in Scripture (or perhaps in some other way). Do what God tells you to do—that's all that ethics needs to think about. Alternately, in an approach that emphasizes outcome one should always seek to discern and then do the most loving thing, following the command of Jesus to love your neighbor as yourself. By contrast to both of these, the third way re-appropriates the classic virtue tradition but invests it with the incorporation of the theological virtues of faith, hope, and love. The point in the third way is to develop character for the sake of the fullness of human flourishing, which fullness includes the love of God.

This chapter takes up each of these approaches in turn.

First Approach: Ethics of Duty

Duty commends itself as the most reasonable way to think about ethics. For to act out of duty pertains to our motivation for action, and ethics does seem to be intimately connected with our inner self being rightly ordered to what we ought to do. The same action may be done by two people, yet if their intentions are different then their actions have different moral worth. Suppose there is a moral rule that able-bodied people should help feeble people crossing the street. Suppose that Able-Bodied Person #1 helps a feeble person cross the street simply because it is her duty to follow that rule; she has no thought of reward for doing so. And suppose that Able-Bodied Person #2 helps another feeble person cross the street out of a calculation that she is likely to get something out of it (maybe an invitation to dinner; maybe an inheritance!). We would think that Able-Bodied Person #1 acted morally, whereas we might well question the moral integrity of Able-Bodied Person #2. Yet, exteriorly, both their actions were the same.

Nevertheless, the rightness of an action, although found in the sacred inner-ness of a person, cannot be in any way peculiar to that person. Rightness of action must also be universal. If it is right for

Able-Bodied Person #1 to follow her duty to help a feeble person cross the street, it would also be right for Able-Bodied Person #2 to do the same thing. Duty, in other words, points to the impersonality that attains to right action: if something is right for Person #1, the same thing is right for any other person who is in the same situation. Duty, thus, points to both the *inwardness* and the *interchangeability* that pertains to ethics.

It was the philosopher Immanuel Kant (1724–1804) who most famously sought a duty-based ethics. Kant wanted an ethics that had the certainty of reason (to keep ethics from being subject to change, emotion, or power-status) and was thus universal. An ethics based on duty, he saw, could meet these requirements: it would be unchanging, unaffected by emotion, and universally applicable to all people (indeed, to all rational beings, whether they be human or not) regardless of their standing or power. Such a duty-based ethic is often termed "deontological," from the Greek word *deon*, "that which is needful, binding, right."

In *The Fundamental Principles of the Metaphysic of Ethics*, Kant points first to the inwardness of morality. "It is impossible to conceive of anything anywhere in the world or even anywhere out of it that can without qualification be called good, except a Good Will."[2] All other good things—from intelligence and beauty to quotidian actions of helping a neighbor—are good only if "qualified" or accompanied by a will that is good. For of course, intelligence can be put to wicked ends, beauty can be used to entrap, and, as we've seen, charitable actions can be done for selfish intent. But a good will needs no further qualification: it is the only thing that is good simply in itself, and it is thus *the* most desirable thing for a person to have.

What, then, does a good will will? It must be something unchanging and universal. Kant provides a brilliant formulation that is universal and interchangeable among all persons (and in that sense, impersonal): "I am never to act otherwise than *so that I could at the same time will that my maxim should become a universal law*."[3] By "maxim" Kant means the rule according to which I am acting in my intentional act. To will that my maxim become a universal law means to will that everyone, in a situation like mine, would act as I am acting. When Kant says "could"—in "I could at the same time will"—he is speaking to strict logical possibility. The duty of a will (and thus what a good will does) is to follow this, as it is called, Categorical Imperative. An example will help make this clear.

Suppose I am visiting someone and I see a twenty-pound note lying under one of his chairs. If I pocket that note while no one is looking, the maxim according to which I am acting is something like, "When unobserved, I may take money that doesn't belong to me." Then to will that that maxim become a universal law would be to say something like, "I hold that, in any case when a person will not be seen doing it, he may take things that do not belong to him." Now Kant's point is to ask simply the following: is it possible or is it self-contradictory to make that last statement? Kant's claim is that if an action is unethical it will be in the end self-contradictory. If I am doing an unethical act, it is impossible for me to will that everyone else act the way that I am acting (or to will that everyone else act according to the maxim that is governing my action). Kant holds, to be specific in terms of this example, that there is something self-contradictory in the idea of willing that all persons may steal when they won't get caught. If all persons steal when they can get away with it, we might very well deem that the whole institution of private property is being undermined; and if there is no private property, then there can be no such thing as stealing.[4]

It is not necessary for us to agree on this particular, and indeed I might be wrong to think that stealing-when-one-doesn't-get-caught cannot be a universal law. All we need to see is the abstraction with which Kant works. For him, morality is not about particular content (e.g., not stealing); it is, rather, about consistency from person to person. Things that are morally right are things that we can will everyone to do who might be in the same situation. And things that are morally wrong are things that, in fact, it is impossible for us to will that everyone might do them.

Deontological Divine Commands

Kant gives us an ethics of duty that is based in the nature of a rational being. In religious ethics of this sort, duty is generally based in the fact of our being creatures (albeit with reason and will). Since we are not God, God can lay duties upon us.

A famous instance of this, two thousand years prior to Kant and half a world away, is in *The Bhagavad Gita*, the canonical text for Hindus. In the *Gita*, the prince Arjuna has to enter a war with family, teachers, and friends on both sides.[5] He does not wish to enter the battle because he does not wish to harm his friends. The god Krishna, with him in his chariot, admonishes him to go to battle and do his duty. But Arjuna states plaintively, "Nothing good can come from slaughtering one's own family in battle" (1.31). He wishes to shun his duty, to pull back from battle and thus symbolically to disengage from life.

Krishna answers with the admonishment that Arjuna must simply do his duty and not be concerned with the outcome. But his words include some religious and philosophical wisdom. "The truly wise do not grieve for the living or the dead," he says, for the reason that all beings are eternal; they do not come to be, and they do not pass away. "Just as within this body the embodied self passes through childhood, youth and old age, so it passes to another body" (2.11, 13). Since the truth is that beings are eternal, we must not be distracted from action by paying any attention to how things turn out. If our duty is to fight in battle, then we must fight. Our duty, in short, is to act as God has placed it upon us to act, without regard for the consequences. Krishna puts this in terms of being "qualified" (think "justified" or "shown to be moral"): "You are qualified simply with regard to action, never with regard to its results." Whether your actions are moral never depends on the results of your actions. "You must be neither motivated by the results of action nor attached to inaction," having "evenness of mind" as to your "success or failure" (2.47-8). That is to say, if we are moral persons then we are to act with "freedom from the results of action," not being bound by whether our actions have done well or good, borne fruit or proved sterile. But we cannot attain this freedom by withdrawing from action (3.4); we have to be engaged with the world while managing to do so with a certain indifference. "Therefore, without attachment, always do whatever action has to be done; for it is through acting without attachment that a man attains the highest.... . [T]he wise should also act ... without attachment, intent upon maintaining the world" (3.19, 25).

So Arjuna, a prince on the field of battle, has a duty that he must fulfill, a duty that is simply there for him (and emphasized to him by the god Krishna). He must fulfill his duty and think not of the consequences of his action. He is not left deprived of all insight whatsoever, for Krishna has taught him about the passage of souls from one body to another. But this insight only reinforces the requirement that he do his duty, regardless of the killings he will inflict. The *Gita* gives us, in this regard, a deontological religious ethics. There are divine commands we have a duty to follow, without regard to the outcome of events.

In Jewish and Christian traditions, the commands of God sometimes have been understood in this deontological way, as duties laid upon us which we must simply fulfill without concern for consequences. There may not be many such commands. Indeed, it seems to me that most of the divine commands in the Bible can be seen to make sense, in that our reason can see the wisdom of following them—can see how these commands safeguard human flourishing. "Do this," the command says, "and your days will be long in the land." Such commands are addressed to our intellect just as much as to our will, and they might well be called edifying commands, in that they aim not only to move us to action but to teach us something. We can see their point, see at least in a partial way the good that they aim to bring about. To follow this sort of divine command is to be concerned with the results of action.

Nonetheless, once we set aside such divine commands as speak to our intellect, there may remain still some commands, albeit perhaps only a small number, that resist our understanding. We just cannot see their point; to follow them we must not consider the result. To these impenetrably opaque commands, then, we can be called to give nothing but the sheer assent of our uncomprehending will.

And if there are any such sheer divine commands in the Bible, surely the strongest candidate is the divine command to Abraham that he sacrifice his son Isaac (Gen. 22.1-19). Abraham had been called by God to become the father of "a great nation" (12.2). He was promised that his descendants would be as innumerable as "the dust of the earth" (13.16) and the stars of the sky (15.5). And yet he had no son by his wife, Sarah, until, when he was a hundred years old, Isaac was born (21.5). Isaac thus is the long-awaited key to the fulfillment of God's promises to Abraham. Thus God's command to Abraham that he sacrifice his son makes no sense. If Abraham is to fulfill this command, he must do so as a matter of duty alone, with no regard—just as Krishna would say—to "the results of action."

Yet even here we may find hints of intelligibility, hints that behind the bald command there is something that might be mulled over by reason—at least the reason of the reader, if not of Abraham at the moment. This command to Abraham is said to be a test (Gen. 22.1). And it is a test that Abraham seems to have passed, for after he all-but-sacrificed his son (having been stopped at the last moment by the abrupt angelic command, "Abraham, Abraham!" [22.11]) he was told: "now I know that you fear God, since you have not withheld your son, your only son, from me" (22.12). The test seems to be a trial between Abraham's fear of God and his love of Isaac. The Jewish scholar Jon Levenson manages to find some deep wisdom at this point. Abraham has to give up Isaac to God who gave Isaac life and who has a role for him in his plan. To fear God is to put those considerations above the old ways of parent and child, ways from which Abraham has already departed, going back to the beginning of his following of God's call. In addition, there is a way of seeing God's mercy and justice reconciled in the trials of righteous folk like Abraham. That Abraham passes the test shows, Levenson says, that God's choice of Abraham was fair and not capricious.[6]

Levenson's work is hardly uncontroversial; he himself is taking aim at Christian interpretations of Abraham's trial as a test of faith. But regardless of one's verdict on his conclusions, Levenson shows that even in this extreme case of a divine command, there may still be something for reason to learn. Which is to say that there may not be any such thing as purely deontological divine commands.

Here is my conclusion. If one is able to find some intelligibility in divine commands (as perhaps Arjuna is given in the belief that all being is eternal and thus action is ultimately unreal yet necessary, and as perhaps we see in Abraham's learning of a new way), then those commands are not sheerly deontological: they are not matters of blind obedience. On the other hand, if divine, sheerly deontological commands do exist, then the point of acting morally is unintelligible, for they amount to precisely, and nothing more, than doing our duty because God tells us to do it.

Kant, by partial contrast, gives duty-ethics a high intelligibility, grounded in the austere consistency of the Categorical Imperative. But this intelligibility is bought at a high price, for it shares with divine deontological commands a necessary indifference to outcome. The sense of discomfort with this conclusion leads us to our next approach to ethics.

Second Approach: Ethics of Outcome

To seek intelligibility in a command is to have our mind turned to the end, the purpose of the command, and away from sheer duty. For many thinkers, the outcome of human action is where we find its moral worth. Theories along this line are broadly called "consequentialist," in that they identify as the heart of morality the maximizing of beneficial consequences, rather than the prizing of a Kantian good will that performs its duty without regard to consequences. An ethical person is one who cares to make things better. Not coincidentally, consequentialist conceptions of ethics flourished hand-in-hand with concern for social betterment in the English-speaking world of the nineteenth century.

In its crude forms, consequentialism has at once an obvious appeal and a troubling weakness. The appeal is simply that, however tenuous the connection might be, morality must have some benefit to human beings. So how things turn out cannot be a matter of moral indifference. But the weakness also is immediately evident. If the moral character of an action is given by its consequences, then it does not matter whether the person acting has a good will or not. Or—at the most—the only goodness to having a good will is that having one makes for better outcomes; a good will, contra Kant, is not good in itself. Similarly, if the outcome is all that matters, then there is no action that, in itself, is right or wrong. Any action we might think of could be, in some circumstance, the right thing to do. Consequentialism, in its crude forms, seems to give permission for many actions that some people, at least, have thought were always and everywhere wrong: things like torture, for example, or rape, or genocide.

The English philosopher John Stuart Mill (1806–73) set forth a nuanced and subtle form of consequentialism in his 1861 book, *Utilitarianism*. Mill defends "utility" as "the foundation of morals" and defines it as "the greatest happiness principle": "actions are right in proportion as they tend to promote happiness; wrong as they tend to produce the reverse of happiness." He defines happiness as pleasure with the absence of pain, and unhappiness as the opposite. He defends this point with the observation that "pleasure and freedom from pain are the only things desirable as ends," for anything else we might desire, we desire either for its inherent pleasure or as a means to advance pleasure and prevent pain.[7]

But here Mill subtly complexifies his argument. Pleasure is not simple hedonism, he says, for it must be pleasure that is appropriate to a human being. "Human beings have faculties more elevated than the animal appetites and, when once made conscious of them, do not regard anything as happiness which does not include their gratification." So a properly human understanding of pleasure must include "pleasures of the intellect, of the feelings and imagination, and of the moral sentiments," and these pleasures must be ranked higher than "those of mere sensation." Properly human pleasure, in other words, is more than the immediate tinglings of carnal delight. True happiness for human beings will include the gratification of our higher qualities. Hence it doesn't matter whether you have a lot of pleasure; what matters, to a human being, is the quality of the pleasures that you have. And the rule for measuring quality is founded in the nature of the human being.[8]

But how can we know what are the pleasures that are truly appropriate to human beings? Mill contends that the hierarchy of human pleasures can be known and identified by people with a certain sort of experience, people who are, he says, "competently acquainted" with the pleasures in question. "Now it is an unquestionable fact," he writes, "that those who are equally acquainted with and equally capable of appreciating and enjoying both [higher and lower pleasures] do give a most marked preference to the manner of existence which employs their higher faculties"— so much so, that they would willingly take on a great deal of discomfort for the sake of the latter. Mill's argument here entails an implicit claim for the epistemic authority had by certain "competently acquainted" persons, as we see in his vivid conclusion to this part of the argument. "It is better to be a human being dissatisfied than a pig satisfied; better to be Socrates dissatisfied than a fool satisfied. And if the fool, or the pig, are of a different opinion, it is because they only know their own side of the question. The other party to the comparison knows both sides."[9]

Now if we are to take the approach of an ethics of outcome—whether in the crude sort of just maximizing pleasure or in a more sophisticated version such as Mill's which distinguishes the happiness that particularly belongs to human beings—we seem to need something like a mathematical formula into which we input the relevant pleasures and pains that would come from various contemplated courses of actions in order to determine which course is the most moral (producing the greatest happiness). As Jean Porter puts it, we need "a convincing standard of commensuration."[10] But opponents of consequentialism (any sort of ethics of outcome) argue that pleasures and pains are not homogeneous. There is no formula in which you can put them together with their pluses and minuses and find which has the best outcome. The problem is clear; a city council cannot decide between spending a sum of money on a park versus spending that money on a school simply by calculating which produces the most happiness.

Yet Mill has anticipated that objection, and he attempts to deflect it by turning again to the epistemic authority of those who understand the various pleasures in question. Mill admits that pleasures and pains are heterogeneous; precisely for that reason, he argues, only the experienced can judge which is greater. "What means are there of determining which is the acutest of two pains, or the intensest of two pleasurable sensations, except the general suffrage of those who are familiar with both? Neither pains nor pleasures are homogeneous, and pain is always heterogeneous with pleasure." Thus: "to decide whether a particular pleasure is worth purchasing at the cost of a particular pain" our only recourse is to "the feelings and judgment of the experienced" who, in fact, according to Mill, "declare the pleasures derived from the higher faculties to be preferable *in kind*."[11]

A final problem for consequentialists is to give some account of the extent of the pleasure that is to be promoted. In a standard formulation, it is "the greatest happiness (or good) of the greatest number." Mill states his view unambiguously: "the utilitarian standard ... is not the agent's own greatest happiness, but the greatest amount of happiness altogether."[12] This means that self-sacrifice, even martyrdom, is moral action, provided that it promotes the overall happiness—and if it doesn't, it's immoral. "A sacrifice which does not increase or tend to increase the sum total of happiness, [utilitarianism] considers as wasted." Yet between a person's own happiness "and that of others, utilitarianism requires him to be strictly impartial as a disinterested and benevolent spectator." Mill at this point explicitly invokes Christianity. "In the golden rule of Jesus of Nazareth, we read the complete spirit of the ethics of utility. 'To do as you would be done by,' and 'to love your neighbor as yourself,' constitute the ideal perfection of utilitarian morality."[13]

Mill's utilitarianism is a sophisticated account of an outcome-based morality. He builds in a nuanced understanding of pleasure. Like Kant, he starts with something that is to be desired in itself, although, whereas for Kant that is a good will, for Mill it is pleasure and the avoidance of pain. And like Kant, he emphasizes an impersonal element. For Kant, impersonality entered through the willingness to universalize the maxim of one's actions. For Mill, it is given by the requirement to seek the overall happiness and to be impartial with regard to one's own. I turn now to examine the Christian element of neighbor-love.

Love Your Neighbor as Yourself

In the previous chapter, when dealing with how Christian beliefs might shape Christian ethics, I used an example that is common to many contemporary urban settings: walking past people who are lying on sidewalks. This situation, I said, could not be interpreted without opening a variety of narratives, not only those of the persons involved but also biblical narratives. We have seen just above that, in defense of his conception of ethics as grounded by utility, Mill said that the ideal of this utilitarian morality was to love your neighbor as yourself. Is it right to understand love of neighbor as a fulfillment of utilitarian ethics?

The sentence appears before us as a command: "you shall love your neighbor as yourself" (Lev. 19.18; cf. Lk. 10.27 and parallels). But being in the form of a command does not make it a deontological command in the sense we saw previously. A command to do one's duty without regard to consequences entails that we must know or be told what that duty is, even if we don't see what good will come of it. Arjuna is to engage in battle; Abraham is to sacrifice Isaac; the Kantian moral agent is to act with the abstract consistency of the Categorical Imperative. A command is elucidating, by contrast, when it is one whose point we can see. If, for instance, the command to engage in battle or to sacrifice Isaac can be understood to advance some human good, then we have moved from blind duty on to a rationally enlightened and informed human action. To take a different example: to honor your parents that your days may be long (Exod. 20.12) is clearly an elucidating command, with the benefit that is stated within the command being an invitation to learn about the importance of living in such ways of reverence that one's days are long, which is in turn, I think, really about having a kind of life that has lasting importance, and about the place of filial piety to that kind of life.

But what, then, is the elucidating quality of the command to love your neighbor as yourself? Whether it has an elucidating quality at all might be questioned, in that Kant also makes reference to the command (along with Jesus' additional command to love one's enemies) as an indication that true morality has nothing to do with acting from one's inclinations; one must instead "do good out of duty, even though no inclination at all impels toward it."[14] The reader here might be tempted to despair as it seems the same scriptural injunction can equivalently support two such disparate ethical approaches as duty and utility.

A way forward is given by some attention to the surrounding narrative. In St. Luke's Gospel, it is a lawyer who, testing Jesus, articulates the love of God and neighbor as the key in the law to inheriting eternal life (10.25-27). The lawyer then tries to justify his having raised a question at all by pointing to something that is not clearly stated by the law: who is my neighbor?

That, I think, is a key to the elucidating character of the command to love one's neighbor. The command has the specificity given by that word "neighbor" (as well as other specificity given by "love" and "as yourself"). But it lays it upon the hearer of the command to determine what is meant by "neighbor." And then, turning to consider the identity of who the neighbor might be (according to this utilitarian reading), the hearer of the command is brought to a consideration of the outcome of his action. He is directed forward to identify his neighbor and to find what he can do to love his neighbor—to maximize his neighbor's happiness.

This, however, is not exactly the trajectory of thought given by St. Luke's Gospel.

Here is how it goes. Immediately after the question "Who is my neighbor?" Jesus tells the parable of the good Samaritan (10.30-36). This parable identifies particular actions of love (seeing the wounded man, tending his wounds, taking him to lodging, arranging for his care) done by a particular man (a Samaritan) to the other particular man who had been attacked and abandoned. But at the end of the parable, Jesus does not ask who was the Samaritan's neighbor. Instead, as I noted in the previous chapter, he asks which person in the parable proved himself a neighbor to the man who had been attacked. In other words, Jesus turns the question upside-down. The command from Leviticus (rightly identified by the questioning lawyer as key to eternal life) that one should love one's neighbor, sheds light on the following specification of ethics: the ethical person proves himself neighbor to others through acts of love in concrete situations at hand. That is to say, it is not the job of the ethical person to identify who his neighbors are; rather, it is his job to prove himself a neighbor.

So we may see the command "Love your neighbor as yourself" as having a specific elucidating quality: fulfillment of it points to the good that one become a neighbor. But can this good be rightly understood, then, as utility? It seems to me that Mill wants to interpret it differently than the line taken in the parable of the good Samaritan, that Mill wants the emphasis to fall upon the "as yourself," so that the command is fulfilled when one acts with indifference to one's own particular good. The utilitarian moralist can then point to the outcome, to the many neighbors whose (properly human) pleasure is increased through moral actions of selfless love of neighbor. This is assuredly a good thing—social improvement is without doubt a goal to be desired—but it is not the good of the character-development of becoming a true neighbor.

To heighten the contrast, let me introduce the reader to a famous book of 1966 whose influence still runs strong. The book is *Situation Ethics: The New Morality*, written by the Episcopal priest Joseph Fletcher. The back cover of the book breathlessly proclaims as a virtue of the book the very problem with utilitarianism that Mill tried to avoid: "The sensational deductions which the author draws ... include the bold statement that any act—even lying, premarital sex, abortion, adultery, and murder—*could* be right, *depending on the circumstances*."[15] Fletcher's "new morality" is a consequentialism that calls, in every situation, for the most loving thing to be done. In what he sets out as a middle way between legalism and antinomianism, traditional moral rules that forbid lying and so forth are to be understood as guidelines that usually work. But in some situations, we need to break the rules in order to serve that which was always the point of the rules, that the most loving thing be done.[16] So Fletcher would interpret the command to love your neighbor as yourself not as a summary of the law[17] but as a higher-level law that can override particulars when they get in the way of love. With regard to the particular biblical command to love the neighbor, Fletcher says we must "do some tinkering" with Scripture and make it plural. For we never meet just one neighbor, but are always dealing with many—as justice, which is nothing but love distributed, requires.[18] Thus Fletcher shows that he does not see a point to the reversal in Jesus' question to the lawyer: "Which of them proved himself a neighbor?" For Fletcher, love of neighbor is a strictly consequentialist morality.

One difficulty is precisely the matter heralded on the back cover: that, pushed to an extreme, an ethics of outcome will find there is nothing that is wrong apart from circumstances. If it seems quaint to find "premarital sex" in that list, the reader might yet pause to wonder about other words that could well be placed there: "ethnic cleansing," say, or my aforementioned "torture." Another difficulty is that situation ethics tends to focus on discrete situations, and thus tends to make ethics into a matter of solving quandaries. With any form of consequentialism, an imponderable question will be the extent of the relevant consequences. If we focus our thought on a particular situation, we may fail to consider how our resolution in this particular will affect future situations, the texture of our society, and our own character. Yet these are important considerations that ethics should not put to the side.[19]

Christian ethics, if it takes its cue from the concern to prove oneself a neighbor, will be unsatisfied with a consequentialist reading of "Love your neighbor as yourself" that focuses on outcome only, and not the self-formative task of becoming as a neighbor. Nor will it interpret that self-formative task as a duty that exists independently of outcome. The third approach to ethics, to which I now turn, puts its focus on the character of the moral agent and on the community and its formative narratives, out of which she has arisen.

Third Approach: Ethics of Excellence

This third approach to ethics often goes by the name of "virtue," and I will often speak of it as "virtue ethics." But this can be misleading, if we think of virtue in a prim-and-proper way. The word in Greek is *areté*, which means "excellence," and that points us in the right direction. Virtue ethics is about being excellent human beings and has a particular line about the way we achieve excellence: it is by the cultivation of the various moral virtues (i.e., moral excellences) through wisdom.

The classic exposition is given in the *Nicomachean Ethics* of Aristotle (384–322 B.C.). The orientation of Aristotle's thought is teleological, meaning that he sees it as natural for us humans to have purposes and aims in everything we do. "Every art and every investigation," he begins, "and likewise every practical pursuit or understanding, seems to aim at some good: hence it has been well said that the Good is That at which all things aim."[20] What is that good? He explores alternatives, and settles on happiness. But what is happiness? Here Aristotle's thought takes a different line from Mill's and Fletcher's. One might think happiness is pleasure or honor, he says. But those are passive things, and real happiness is active. In fact (and here is the substance of his definition), "happiness is activity of the soul in accordance with complete virtue throughout life."[21] He emphasizes "activity," since happiness is found in what we do. For Aristotle, a sleeping man is not happy, nor is a dead man; nor would we consider happy someone who was acting in an involuntary way on account of medicines or hypnosis. Happiness is a feature of being fully alive. By "soul," Aristotle means our liveliness; in the technical terms of his philosophy, the soul is the "form" of a living being. By "virtue," he means (as I said above) something we might better translate as "excellence." To act with virtue is for a human being to act with excellence, (as we might say) to do well as a human being, to flourish. Happiness is connected with complete human virtue in that we might do well in some aspect of our humanity and yet not be happy. For instance, we might be excellent as a swimmer, but not happy; we might excel in business management, be an expert in plant classification, or perform beautiful works on the harp. But unless we have excellence overall as a human being, happiness will not be ours. Similarly and finally, Aristotle adds that it needs to be in a complete life. By this he cannot mean that we must reach the end of our life before we can be happy (for that would be the old dismal Catch-22: you can't be happy now if there might be misfortune later, but the only way not to have possible misfortune in your future is to be dead, and if you're dead, you can't be happy anyway!). He means something more ordinary, that happiness takes a span of time, more than a moment, more than a day. You see happiness when you see someone who is good in human activities stretching over a variety of situations and moments of life.

That happiness is an activity is a pivotal point for Aristotle and for virtue ethics generally, and yet it might not be immediately obvious. To bring out the point, a number of philosophers employ the thought-experiment of an experience-machine. Imagine that there is a machine into which your body could be placed, and then, once in the machine, you will get to "experience" anything and everything that you want. If you want ravishing sexual experiences, they will be yours; if you want to experience the fame of a rock star, you've got it; if you want to become a brilliant scholar who can write in eight languages, read fourteen, and solve complicated linguistic problems, that you will be. Anything you want, you will get to have the "experience" of having it. However, none of these experiences will really happen; you, in the experience-machine, will think that they are happening, but in fact you will not be doing any of them. You will simply be plugged-in (not unlike the humans in the "Matrix" films). Nonetheless, *you will not know* that the experiences are unreal; you will think that you are having them. And then, after many years, you will have a painless death. The question is: would you enter the experience-machine? On the one hand, if you do so, you will never again make a free decision in the real world. On the other hand, you will not know that that is your state, and you will enjoy any and every pleasant experience of whatever sort you wish for the rest of your life. What will you choose?[22]

The thought-experiment makes two related points about happiness and experience. First, any reluctance to enter the machine points to our understanding that happiness is more than passively-received pleasures, even pleasures of a very refined sort; happiness has an intrinsic connection with activity. And second, quite apart from happiness, our reluctance points to a sense that real experience is good in its own right, even if it is not pleasurable. As Mill said, it is better to be a human being unsatisfied than a pig satisfied. It is better to live a real human life with its uncertainties and challenges, than to live a less-than-human life with full contentment. But with virtue ethics, unlike Mill's utilitarian ethics of outcome, the emphasis is placed on the right-functioning of the human being.

So Aristotle emphasizes that happiness is *activity* in accordance with human virtue or excellence. Aristotle also has insight into the nature of virtue. In general terms, a virtue is an acquired disposition of the soul to choose the mean appropriately. We speak primarily of persons as having virtue; for while we may speak of an act as virtuous, that sense of virtue is derivative of the primary one, which belongs to character. You are an excellent (virtuous) human being if you act in a characteristic way. That characteristic manner of acting is to choose, and to do so without great struggle, the appropriate mean for the situation at hand. By "mean," Aristotle has in mind an acquired disposition of character to avoid opposite extremes that encumber human flourishing. But this is highly general speech; it will be clearer if we make it particular.

Courage is one of the virtues: it is an acquired disposition not to be frozen into inaction in the face of something fearful or dangerous. So we might think of courage as the opposite of timidity. But courage is also opposed to rashness, which is an excessive disregard for danger, a moving impulsively and unwisely into danger rather than acting appropriately. Thus courage is opposed to both extremes, timidity and rashness. It is, in that sense, a "mean."

It is not easy to acquire virtues. They cannot be learned from books, but take practice. And the process is irreducibly circular. If you want to be a courageous woman, then you must act like a courageous woman. But there is a difference between "acting like" you have a virtue and actually having it. The process of acquiring virtues involves apprenticeship and practice, intentional experience. One must take into account one's own native and unformed disposition, which is never exactly the same as another person's. You might be constitutionally predisposed towards rashness; and if so, then in your case the development of courage will require a particular movement in the direction of timidity, so that things come out balanced in the end. By contrast, I might be more timid by nature, and thus need to act in a way that, for you, would be rash. We both want to end up at the mean: with the disposition to act, as our second nature and without great difficulty, in an excellent way that involves courage and all the other virtues, so that we can be excellent, flourishing human beings, which is to say, happy.

The *Nicomachean Ethics* is divided into ten books. Scholars think that the received manuscript has been pieced together from other things that Aristotle wrote; certainly it has a looseness of organizational structure to it. Be that as it may, the opening and the closing of the *Ethics* make it clear that it is but the first half of a larger work. The second half is known as the *Politics*, and in it Aristotle takes up the question of the conditions for human beings to live together in governed societies. If we see the *Ethics* and the *Politics* together, we see something important about Aristotle's vision. The human being cannot have happiness alone. The development of virtue and the quest for an excellent human life are not undertakings for individuals, but for persons who are members of governed communities.

Students who read the *Ethics* are sometimes surprised to learn of this intimate connection, in Aristotle's thought, with politics. They may also be surprised to find that two books of the *Ethics* (VIII and IX) are given over to the topic of friendship. But friendship, for Aristotle, is an absolutely necessary element of the ethical, and thus happy, life. We don't acquire virtues so as to live in glorious isolation and indifference to others. Later in this book, a chapter is given over to friendship. For in my view there can be no guidance in Christian ethics that does not give friendship a key place.

A Sports Analogy

Each of the three approaches to ethics has a grasp on something essential. Ethics involves, on some basic level, the adherence to given rules even when we do not understand them. This deontological element points to the inwardness of ethics, that goodness has to do with having something like a pure intention or, as Kant would have it, a Good Will. It also points to the universality of morality: what is right for me to do would be right for anyone else in my situation to do, and conversely for what is wrong. Nonetheless, ethics is about real goods in the actual world we live in, so it cannot be a matter of indifference to us whether the actual world is a good world or not. Granted that the outcome of things cannot be the sole determinant of whether the actions that led up to them were morally correct (we will not go so far as that), yet nonetheless, how things turn out is some part of the point of it all. We may put it this way: indifference to results is not a morally defensible posture.

Yet the results of moral action are not limited to the general effect of our actions in the world. They also include the effect of our actions upon ourselves, how what we choose to do shapes us as moral characters. Virtue ethics rightly points in this direction, insisting that the happiness which is our goal is not something static and external but the activity of the moral agent herself.

Suppose I were to stand before a classroom and say that, for the past two weeks, I have not committed adultery. While my students look blankly at me, I continue by averring that I also have not murdered anyone. Nor, in the past two weeks, have I committed theft. Indeed, I have not lied under oath either. At some point, my students will reply something like this. "It's good that you haven't done any of those bad things for the past two weeks, but it really isn't very impressive. It doesn't mean you're a good person."

And they would be right. Following the rules, particularly the negative rules ("Thou shalt not..."), does not make one a moral person. If you don't follow the rules, you have failed to be a moral person. But if you do follow the rules, that's still not enough to make you a moral person.

Suppose I then go on to say that I've given away lots of money, that last week I also gave time to a neighbor who needed my help, that I am working on a book that may guide people to live better lives and understand what they're doing. They might be more impressed now; at least their professor is doing some good things. But if they are frank with me, they will say, "Even though you've done all those good things, it doesn't mean you're a good person."

And they would be right. I could do all sorts of things that make the world a better place, and still be a bad character. Something else is needed.

So now I draw a rectangle on the chalkboard. "That," I say to my students, "is a soccer field." (I say "soccer" because my students are Americans.) "Now suppose you are a player in that game. Suppose you know all the rules, not only in your head, but in your body, so that you never break any of the rules. Are you a good player?"

The answer is, not necessarily. Indeed, you could follow the rules at all times and still be a lousy player. As far as I can tell, a completely inept soccer player like me could just stand still in the middle of the field while the game bustles and runs all around me and thus succeed in not breaking any rules. But for all my innocence of rule-breaking, I would be a lousy player nonetheless.

"Second step," I continue with my students. "Suppose you are a player whose entire focus is on getting your score as high as you can. So every time you can, you kick the ball straight towards the goal. Does this make you a good player?" And the answer is again no, although there will be some debate on this point. Some people will say that getting the highest score you can is the point of the game, while others will say that, if you focus exclusively on the score, you won't pay attention to other things that are needed, things like teamwork and practice. Although not everyone will agree, a number of them will say that there is a difference between getting the highest score possible and playing the best game you can.

And so we come to the point. We need the rules to establish the boundaries, to give us definitions, so that we can say what counts as playing the game. And we need goals because we are playing the game for a certain output, namely, scoring. But more than rules and goals, to play the game well we need to have the skills and dispositions of good players.

And then to make the analogy explicit: There are actions, committed by human beings, that simply aren't human actions at all; they are like moves that fail to be moves in the soccer game. It isn't playing soccer to pick up the ball with your hands. And it isn't, as it were, "playing the human game" to commit adultery or to murder. Adultery, murder, and the like are actions that human beings can and do commit and yet are not really human actions.

And you can have a high score at the end of the game, just as you can do a lot of good in your life, without it having been a good game or a good life.

What makes it a good game is that it is being played well, which is so much more than being played within the boundaries, and so much richer than having a good score at the end. To play well, in soccer, is to move with strength and elegance, to act creatively, to work well as an individual on a team, to think nimbly on your feet. And to play "the human game" well, to live a happy life, is to act with those virtues that display a human being in flourishing mode.

The point of the analogy is to get my students thinking, to raise some questions and open up some lines of inquiry. Is there indeed such a thing as "playing the human game well"?

From such thoughts, the structure of the remainder of this Guide follows readily. In the next chapter I lay out a Christian account of the principal virtues involved in full human flourishing. I turn in the following chapter to how the virtues get put into play: the excellence of "good sense," the ability to make good decisions, and the difference made by the virtues that God gives us, especially charity. The final two chapters address corollary topics. The first is friendship, a matter of suspicion in some theology, and yet the culmination of virtue. Can we have a robust theological understanding of friendship? Finally, since virtue ethics exalts the capabilities of flourishing human beings, what place then does it have for those who are disabled, particularly persons with mental disabilities? If you don't have the capacities to develop virtues, does virtue ethics exile you to a sub-human state? Therefore this Guide concludes with what Christian ethics has to say about being a person, ending at the deep point where ethics and theology, humanity and God, are one.

*   *   *

Notes for Further Reading

With regard to the nature of divine commands as found in the Bible, Ellen Charry argues that all biblical commands have been wrongly assumed to be voluntarist orders, peculiar to a given situation and addressing the will with the point of testing sheer obedience. She demonstrates, to the contrary, that the vast majority of biblical commands are nonvoluntarist, offering guidance that is understandable to the human mind and thereby being the occasion to cultivate wisdom. Behind this distinction is the old debate (e.g., between the medieval voluntarists and Aquinas) whether something is wrong simply because God forbids it, or if God forbids those things which we can then see and understand to be wrong. See Ellen T. Charry, *God and the Art of Happiness* (Grand Rapids, Mich.: Eerdmans, 2010), especially ch. 8, "Divine Commands." As the reader will have seen, I have doubts about whether *any* divine commands are simply voluntarist (in my terminology, "deontological divine commands").

A selection of key passages of Kant's *Fundamental Principles of the Metaphysic of Ethics*, in a contemporary translation, may be found in Cooper ed. *Ethics: The Classic Readings*, 166–80. Mill's key chapter 2 of *Utilitarianism* is reprinted with only slight abridgement in the same volume. Thus with Cooper's book the student may read the key passages from Kant, the *Gita*, and Mill that are discussed in this chapter.

For a breathtakingly comprehensive rebuttal of situation ethics from the Protestant side, see Paul Ramsey, "The Case of Joseph Fletcher and Joseph Fletcher's Cases," in his *Deeds and Rules in Christian Ethics* (New York: Charles Scribner's Sons, 1967), 145–225. Ramsey, who had many students who went on to prominence in the ethical field, was nonetheless thoroughly a controversialist of his age. Reading first Fletcher's short book *Situation Ethics* and then Ramsey's almost equally-long essay is to be dropped back a half-century in time, with the thrill of finding oneself in the midst of titanic struggles at the very time of their unfolding. The student can learn much from the experience.

CHAPTER FOUR

How to Succeed as a Human Being

What the human good is, what human excellence is, and what the virtues are

Good Apples and Good People

The adjective "good" functions differently than the adjective "red."[1] If I say you are holding a red apple and that you are also wearing red socks, I mean that both your apple and your socks are the same color. If I add that I've caught you in your red socks stealing that red apple red-handedly, I mean that your face is (or ought to be) flush with the shame of being caught out at doing a wrong, and thus your face too shares the color "red." (I don't mean that your hands are red with your victim's blood; although, who knows what you had to do to get that red apple red-handedly?)

But if, to the contrary, I say you are holding a good apple and you are also wearing good socks, I do not mean that the apple and the socks have something in common. A good apple is tasty and a delight to eat; good socks are neither tasty nor a delight to eat. If I make you eat your sock it would not be because it was a good sock, nor would I be a particularly good person to make you do so. The redness of an apple is like unto the redness of socks, cheeks, and other red things. The goodness of an apple is not at all like the goodness of socks and other good things.

An apple is good, if I may risk putting it oddly, when it is succeeding at being an apple. And a bad apple is one that somehow falls short of success at appleness. A good sock does what socks are supposed to do, and (for instance) doesn't have too many holes, won't bunch up in my shoe, and so forth. If I said to you that I had a bad apple, you wouldn't know from that information alone how to picture it; you wouldn't know what made it bad. It might be rotten on one side, or it might have a worm inside it, or it might have grown incorrectly and be too fibrous to eat. If, however, I went on to say that my apple was bad because it didn't keep my feet warm, you would rightly turn your attention from the apple to me. You might well ask: Is Austin crazy? Has he confused the word "apple" with the word "sock"? Perhaps he doesn't understand English?

What all this points to is the peculiarity of that adjective "good." "Good" means that the noun which it modifies is what it is supposed to be, that it is living up to its nature (or, if you prefer, its definition). A good apple succeeds at being an apple. A good sock is living up to what we expect in socks.

Similarly, I say, a good human being is succeeding at being a human being. But what in the world could that mean—to "succeed at being human"? Do we have a standard against which to measure humanness? Human beings, after all, are very much different from apples and socks. Apples and socks have no say in what they are or what they become, but we humans are all the time deciding what we'll be and do. Apples, we might say, have a given nature, shaped over time by the forces of evolution and the practices of cultivation and perhaps, most recently in history, of genetic manipulation. Still, although their nature may have changed over time, for any given apple here today there is a nature against which we can say whether it's a good apple or not. And socks are not natural things, so they don't have natures, but still we make them with expectations of what they are good for, and we can quite appropriately say whether a sock lives up to expectations—whether it's good or bad. But people are vastly different. We don't have a nature that simply has its way with us; we have to be nursed and loved and disciplined and guided in order to grow up; we need education and friends and laws and lots of other things that are given to us, or else any of us will most likely fail to be very much of a human being. We are somewhat like apples in that some element of unconscious nature is given to us, and we are somewhat like socks in that others have their way with us in our nurture and maturation and then throughout the rest of our life; yet there is also an individual element to each of us, something "interior" that goes beyond the givens of apples and socks. This further element is what is spoken of when people speak of such things as reason, will, consciousness, conscience, and the like.

Aquinas says (and according to Jean Porter it is the key to understanding his ethics) that what makes us humans distinctive is that we can rationally grasp our human end.[2] That is, we don't move by sub-rational or irrational nature towards our humanity; our humanity is something that lies before us as a task to be undertaken. But to say this entails that Aquinas must have a notion of the human end, of what is good for human beings. He must, that is, have an account of what a good human being is. And for that, he must have an account of what the true human good is.

What's Good for Human Beings

Thomas Aquinas (c. 1225–74) is one of the two most influential Christian theologians in the West (the other being Augustine, his predecessor by some eight centuries). His importance for us is his account of the human virtues in the moral life. Aquinas brought the thought of Aristotle on the virtues into a Christian framework. Like Aristotle, Aquinas is teleological; he begins with the fact (as he sees it) that all things act towards ends, and thus there is an end that is the goal for human beings. That end is happiness, which is the condition of being intimately united with God in the beatific vision. But God, in Aquinas's understanding, has created things that are not himself. These created things—this created world—can be understood to a large degree (if not ultimately) on their own terms. Thus we can understand the human being as having, besides its ultimate end in God, created and creaturely ends. There is a created good for the human being, as for every other being.

The created good for any being is, in the end, nothing else but that being itself. This is because anything that exists is, insofar as it exists, good. The writer of the first creation account in Genesis seems to have this perspective, in that he uses as a repeated refrain "God saw that [what he had made] was good" and then, at the conclusion of creation, "God saw everything that he had made, and indeed, and it was very good" (Gen. 1.4, 12, 18, 21, 25, 31). So in a basic sense, "to be" is the same thing as "to be good." Yet in another sense, things can fall short, so that goodness is the ideal or the end, the perfection, of the particular being. An apple is good, in the minimal sense, if it succeeds at being an apple instead of being dirt. In the other sense, it is a good apple if it does not fall short in its appleness.

So following this line of thought, to know the good for a human being is nothing else but to know what is a human being, with the understanding that some human beings fall short. Indeed, here a Christian understanding makes a particular substantive contribution to the argument. For a Christian, there has been in fact one fully human being, namely, Jesus.[3] He "fully reveals man to man himself," in the remarkable formulation, previously noted, of the Second Vatican Council.[4] So the task for the theologian is, using both reflection upon actual human beings and the insights of revelation, to attempt to articulate what the human good is.

Aquinas has done just that, and (to jump to his answer) it involves four things: self-preservation, procreation, living in society, and knowing the truth about God.[5] These are, in Aquinas's estimation, the fundamental human inclinations, arranged in ascending order of importance. Like all creatures, human beings strive to continue to exist; self-preservation is thus the first and most fundamental inclination. Like all living creatures, humans seek to reproduce themselves; thus, procreation is another fundamental inclination, but laid on top of self-preservation. Living in society marks the human as an essentially social being. And knowing God is the highest end we have, and thus the inclination most elevated in our nature.[6]

Correspondingly, the human good involves all these elements; to succeed at being a human being will involve grasping with one's intellect this complex, four-fold good and shaping one's life towards this good appropriately. It is important to see that these elements are not independent of each other, but are hierarchically arranged. By itself, any one of them gives permission for action. That is, apart from other considerations, an action that leads towards any element of the complex human good is by that very fact morally justified. But their hierarchical structure means that the higher goods should be preferred to the lower. Thus, if there is a situation in which self-preservation is in conflict with procreation, the latter good is to be preferred. One might think of a parent who has to choose between feeding himself and feeding his child. Normally, there is no need to justify eating—it is necessary for self-preservation. But if my eating is at the expense of my child's, then the good of the child (the good of self-reproduction) has precedence. Similarly, if either self-preservation or procreation conflicts with social life, or if the goods of any of these first three conflict with the knowledge of God, the higher good should prevail.

Furthermore, the natural permission to seek these goods as elements of the human good also entails that others should not harm us by taking away or preventing us from obtaining these goods. Working from knowledge of God backwards, they entail: respect and protection of religious freedom, of social association, of marriage (the context, for Aquinas, for human reproduction), and of life itself. As protections against harm, the stronger prohibitions apply to the more basic goods, with the most fundamental being the respect and protection of life.

This has practical consequences in our postlapsarian world. Of course, if human nature were not fallen from its created goodness—if there were no sin in the world—the four human goods would work harmoniously together. But in the world as it is, there are often forced choices. So if it proved necessary to infringe either religious freedom or social association, then, since infringing social association is more strongly prohibited, social association would warrant the stronger defense. Likewise, marriage would warrant a stronger defense than either of those two, and life itself would warrant the strongest defense of all. If necessary for the good of social association, a religious group may be required to have a permit for a parade or a bonfire, even if such regulation impedes the free exercise of religion; the institution of marriage is protected even if it should have a negative impact on social association; and a person's immunity from assault protects him from spousal abuse, even if that immunity should weaken the institution of marriage.

These four elements give us, in outline, Aquinas's account of the human good. Within the parameters of this Guide there is not space to defend his account at length. It strikes this author as a fairly reasonable account. With the goods of self-preservation and reproduction, it takes seriously the connection of humans to the rest of creation. With the good of social intercourse, it points to the human distinctiveness and the importance of socially-given constructs such as language. And by including the fourth good, it points to our ultimate end as having intimacy with God.

But how is that complex of goods to be attained? If that is what the human good is, then how do we play the human game well—how do we succeed at being human beings? To address such questions, we turn to the virtues.

Human Excellence

There are four cardinal virtues (or excellences): temperance, courage, justice, and good sense. These are called "cardinal" because on them hinges the moral life. (The Latin *cardo* originally meant a door hinge.) To speak of four virtues only is to speak conveniently; there are, in fact, as many virtues as there are types of situations in the face of which human beings act.[7] In fact, if you were to look at the virtues as Aristotle discusses them in the *Nicomachean Ethics*, you would not find this simple scheme of four.[8] Nonetheless, it does have a logic to commend it.

First we note that the human being has "affections" or "passions." These are our desires and fears, our almost-innate and sub-rational responses to things and events in the world around us. We may love, seek, avoid, fear, or dread; we may become passionate or ecstatic in self-forgetfulness of the moment, or we may react with coldness and indifference or even hostility. But all these multitudes of particular affections can be divided into two groups: attractions and aversions, corresponding respectively to things to which we are drawn by our passions and things from which we turn away on account of their danger or difficulty.

Both of these types of affections have something to learn. The attractive affections—those that are drawn towards things—need to learn *temperance*, which is to say, they need to be taught by reason to desire particular goods only in the right way at the right time. Similarly, the affections that turn away from danger or difficulty need to learn *courage*, need, that is, to learn from reason not to shirk action when action is required, to act neither rashly nor timidly.

Temperance and courage are the two cardinal virtues for the affections. They are virtues that pertain to the human being considered in herself, in the way she responds to the world. But since human beings are also social, there is a virtue of living well with other people, the virtue of *justice*. This is a virtue not of the affections but of the will. It amounts to treating others fairly so that human beings can live well together.

The fourth cardinal virtue is a virtue of the intellect, an excellence specifically of the human decision-making capacity. It is traditionally called *prudence*, but (following Herbert McCabe) we might prefer to call it *good sense*, to emphasize its practicality and to avoid the inference that it has principally to do with being careful (the usual connotation today of "prudent"). Indeed, one with the virtue of good sense might well make a dramatic and courageous decision that was decisive and life-changing, the very opposite of what we would call cautious or prudent (in customary use).

The virtues work together; in fact, truly to have any one of them requires that you have them all. Both temperance and courage are needed if one's affections are to be rightly ordered. But the operation of these virtues of the affections requires that they be guided by the virtue of good sense. It takes good sense to know what temperance or courage should be in a particular situation (and given your own personal constitution). To advert to the Aristotelian term, it is by good sense that a person finds the correct "mean" that is temperance or courage (remembering that, as a virtue, good sense itself is also a "mean" of sorts). Furthermore, since you can't navigate through any situation without dealing with other people, justice must continually inform your actions. Justice, for instance, makes sure that your affections are ordered, through temperance and courage, to a right regard for the fundamental equality of people.[9]

In the previous chapter it was said that a virtue is something like a second nature, an almost-instinctive way of acting, an acquired ability to "play the human game well." What this chapter has so far presented is an account of what the good is, and in particular an account of the human good based on the four basic human inclinations, and some further thought about the logic of organizing the virtues in terms of four that are cardinal. I turn now to the characteristics of the virtues, particularly temperance, courage, and justice. Justice will require extended attention, for it grounds the stringent prohibitions of wrongful acts such as murder. But in the end we cannot act well simply by avoiding wrongful action. We need the ordering of all the virtues given by the excellence of good sense. And we need, in addition, the Christian change brought about by the theological virtues, particularly charity. These will be the subject of Chapter 5.

Excellences of the Affections: Temperance and Courage

The affective virtues (along with justice, the excellence of the will) are sometimes called "moral" virtues.[10] The excellences of temperance and courage are needed for effective action. For if a human being is to be a good agent in the world, she must be someone who is able to sustain a course of activity over time.

Consider a few of the varieties of intemperance. Someone that we would call an angry person—not someone who happens to be angry on occasion, but one who is characteristically angry in the face of all sorts of situations—is someone who tends to get in her own way. She is habitually angry; she has no regard to the just proportioning of her anger to the matter at hand. You might look at her and wish that she didn't get angry so much. You can see that her anger keeps her from forming correct judgments, and thus she isn't able to be as successful in her undertakings as she could otherwise be.

A glutton, who is intemperate but in a different way from the angry person, is someone who lacks (we might say) "self-control" around food and drink. His gluttonous behavior will exacerbate underlying dispositions of his physical constitution. He is more likely to become a diabetic, for instance, than a temperate person. (Of course, some diabetics have always been temperate with food and drink, and some gluttons never develop diabetes.) We can see that the glutton risks undermining his health, and thus his ability to carry out his projects. His gluttony works against his ability to act effectively in the world—it works against his success as a human being.

Or consider a sexual libertine. His frequent changes of sexual partners means he is likely not to have the strengths and powers needed either to grow in a long-term relationship or to provide the continuity needed to rear children successfully.

These quick instances point to an important truth. Temperance, rightly understood as an excellence, is more about what you are able to do than what you do not do. A temperate person, in contrast to an angrily tempestuous one, is able to carry out her deeper intentions and be successful in her enterprises. A temperate person, in contrast to a glutton, is more likely to enjoy length of life and the full operation of his faculties. A temperate person, in contrast to the sexual libertine, can enjoy maturation in a relationship that extends over time and may in addition be able to guide children into the possibility of excellent living.

So any picture of temperance as a prune-faced negativity is quite the opposite of reality. Aristotle places temperance as the mean between self-indulgence and insensibility. A temperate person rightly values the passion that is anger, but only gets angry when it is right to do so (in the face of injustice). A temperate person is not insensitive to the pleasures of food and sex; indeed, he appreciates them as much as, and perhaps in truth more than, other people. But these desires, like all desires, are subsumed in temperance in a rational way so that they are directed to the truly human good.

Courage, which is sometimes called "fortitude" (the Latin is *fortitudo*), is the complementary virtue to temperance. It has to do with the right ordering of the aversive affections that would keep us from doing what is dangerous or hard. With courage, one finds the correct mean between timid inaction and rash but irrational action. Just as with temperance, we could consider instances of people who lack the excellence of courage, who either timidly fail to act as they should, or who rashly act without reason. A sad story was once told me of a friend of a teenager in my parish. He was, with other friends, driving at night on the roof of an empty, elevated parking lot. They were seeing how fast they could drive. None of them wanted to be seen as a coward. And in rashness—that false simulacrum of courage—this young man drove his car over the edge of the lot and plunged to his death.

Jean Porter offers as a rough definition of the affective virtues the following: they are "qualities of character which are characterized by actions that exhibit self-control in situations in which one is tempted by desires (in the case of temperance) or aversion, especially fear (with reference to fortitude), to act contrary to one's overall aims or commitments."[11] But then she asks if "self-control" is the right way to think of these virtues. And of course it is not: if a virtue becomes something like second nature to us, we won't be "controlling" ourselves when we exercise a virtue, we will be simply being ourselves. Most of us, however, never achieve perfection in the virtues (which is to say, most of us don't play the human game well all or perhaps even most of the time). We might be such that we tend to do the virtuous thing, but it takes effort on our part. That would be self-control! Our inclinations are not yet virtuously ordered to our "overall aims or commitments" (which would be in accord with the human good). But, in our actions, we tend to do the right (virtuous) thing. We tend to do temperate and courageous actions, despite our inclinations. That means we aren't virtuous, but we act virtuously. Such a person is called "continent." We could also imagine (indeed we might be) a person whose inclinations are not virtuously ordered and who tries to do the virtuous thing but who then tends to fail. So he doesn't act virtuously, but still he tried. We could call such a person "incontinent," to distinguish him from the vicious person who not only has disordered inclinations but doesn't even try to order them.[12]

To grow in virtue, then, is to move up the continuum from viciousness to incontinence and then through continence up, finally, to virtue or excellence itself. In so doing, one grows in the measure of one's success at being a human being.

But the human being is not only an individual whose affections need to learn excellence. She is a social being, and her ability to function well as a human being depends on how well she lives with others. Not only her affections but also her will must learn to be excellent if she is to be so herself.

Excellence of the Will: Justice

How can we see that the virtue of justice is the excellence involved in living well with others? Temperance and courage are needed so that an individual is able to carry out her purposes, not being led astray by unruly affections. But the will also needs to function excellently for a person to flourish as a human being: and the excellence of the will is what is called justice.

It is a complex topic, justice; Aquinas's treatment of it is longer than his treatment of any other virtue, extending from Question 58 to Question 122 of *Summa theologiae* II-II. But fundamentally it has to do with equality. Aristotle puts it almost mathematically as a matter of giving to the other the equal of what the other has given to you.[13] And although the notion of equality is hardly a simple one, it does seem to permeate our notions of justice, even to the iconography of the blind female figure of Justice holding balanced scales.[14]

This respect for fundamental human equality, at the heart of justice, needs to be shown forth in actions that, as Porter puts it (developing Aquinas's view), "embody right relations among individuals, or between the individual and the community."[15] The untutored will already aims at the good of the person (as the person sees it); so, unlike the affections, the will doesn't need anything in order to seek the person's own good. By contrast, the virtues of temperance and courage were necessary to bring their subject-matter, the affections, in line with the overall good of the person. Justice orients the will towards right relationships with others. A just person has such excellence that it is now her character, her sustained intention as exhibited in particular actions, rightly to interrelate with other persons, having a will that considers, thanks to its excellence in justice, not only the overall good of the individual, but that of others. By the standards of justice, "true temperance and fortitude can be distinguished from incomplete or counterfeit forms of these virtues."[16]

Questions will complicate this picture, however, as soon as we push for specificity concerning the notion of equality, which we are taking as central to the notion of justice. How does respect for the fundamental equality of all people play out in questions where there seems to be some conflict between the good of particular individuals and the common good of all? How do we weigh one individual against another, or particular individuals against society as a whole? On the one hand, each human being is a social being. We need communities not only for our physical support but also as places in which we can develop our skills and think together. We figure things out, often, by talking with one another. Language, as I've said before, is there (like the various societies to which we belong) before we appear on the scene. The knowledge that is passed on to us, and language itself, and all the things we mean by "culture"—these are necessary for any of us to be who we are. In these various ways, the community seems more important than the individual, and the common good more important than that of any single person.

Nonetheless, for Aquinas and for the theological tradition of the virtues generally, the individual can in a sense outweigh society. We see this, for instance, in the responsibility to take care of oneself (often derived from the biblical command to love one's neighbor *as oneself*, but also derivable by reason alone: if you are to be an excellent member of any community, you have the responsibility to undertake appropriate self-care). Furthermore, in the Christian tradition, each human being is understood to be, potentially, a friend of God—and the good of knowing God is the highest of all the goods.

So the common good seems to have precedence over individuals, and yet every individual has such value that he seems to be more important than society. This paradox of the fundamental equality of persons is built into the higher-level human goods of living in society and knowing God. We humans are, as it were, social individuals. But beyond the mere statement of this paradox of our nature, we can achieve some further specification about our fundamental equality if we consider certain species of wrongful actions, namely, those actions that are always wrong, always an affront to justice. Murder is one such action.

Murder: Always an Offense against Justice

But what is murder? As a matter of objective description, there are actions in which one human being kills another. Some of these actions are morally justified homicides; the others are classified as murder. How can we tell the difference between the two? It won't do to stipulate that murder is unjustified killing. We need to be able to state why it is unjustified. In what lies the injustice of those homicides that are classified as murder?

I note, first, that before one can know that a murder has been committed one must know something of the narrative that surrounds the action. There is a story to be told here, and if it is a story of murder, then both the killer and the one killed will fit into the story in ways that are defined and describable. And conversely, if it is a justified homicide, the two persons' narratives will have met specifiable conditions.

As Aquinas lays it out, there are two conditions that are necessary for a killing to be a justifiable homicide. First, the killing must be done by an authorized state agent—a soldier, a public executioner, a member of the police, or some other authorized person. And second, the person killed must be a victim who, by his own prior actions, has "forfeited the immunity from harm guaranteed to all members of a just community through his own free action of grievous aggression against the community or some individual."[17] Both of these conditions must be met for a homicide to be justifiable. Thus, to kill an innocent is always murder. Also, for a private person, not authorized by the state, to kill is always murder (even if the victim is not innocent). Killing in self-defense, however, may be justifiable homicide if there was immediate need to repel the assailant and recourse to a state agent was not possible. In such a case, we may think of the person defending herself as implicitly authorized by the state; however, after the event, it will be necessary to see that she had no reasonable alternative. A trained markswoman, for instance, would be expected to aim the bullet to debilitate rather than kill her assailant.

Murder, thus, is a kind of action that can be clearly described and objectively verified. It is always wrong for a private individual to kill another, and it is always wrong to kill an innocent (in the precise sense of one who has not grievously assaulted the community or one of its members). We can tell if a murder has been committed by investigating this narrative context of a given homicidal action. The context points us to the interrelations of individuals and the community. Each individual has a given presumption of immunity from harm; the community cannot take away his life unless he has done something grievously wrong. But if he has committed a wrong, it is the community, with its priority over the individual, who alone may take his life.

One may disagree with this account at some point or other. One may, for instance, disagree that the state should ever exercise capital punishment. Or one may think that the conditions of modern warfare or the phenomena of terrorism require the justification of the killing of innocents in certain situations. For my part,

I believe the state should do away with capital punishment if it can, but whether it can is a culturally-located judgment of political good sense, not a fundamental matter of injustice. And I believe that military actions should never aim at the terrorization of peoples or the direct infliction of death upon noncombatants, and yet the knowledge that noncombatants will be killed or likely killed in a contemplated military action does not make that action unjust (although, if the civilian harm is great and the likely military benefit slight, it would likely be unjust to proceed). You may disagree. But note that our disagreement then would be over the definition of what constitutes wrongful homicide (i.e., murder). You would be arguing for additional criteria for justifiable homicide, beyond the two given (an agent of state doing the killing, and the victim not being innocent). We would not be disagreeing over whether there is such a thing as an action of wrongful homicide that is describable and verifiable.

Here is how the point is made by Herbert McCabe, in an illustration from the late 1960s. Note how he works through a multitude of descriptions of the act in question:

> Take the case of the officer of the Saigon regime who returned home recently to find that his wife and child had been killed, presumably by a member of the National Liberation Front. Various descriptions could be given of the behaviour of the man who killed the officer's child. He was perhaps punishing the officer for atrocities he had committed in the past, he was discouraging others from supporting the corrupt policies of the Saigon government, he was helping to liberate the Vietnamese people, he was killing this child, he was firing his gun in this direction ... and so on. Evidently there are an indefinite number of such descriptions. Now if you hold, for example, that the deliberate killing of children is absolutely wrong, then you hold that no matter what else occurs in the list, so long as it contains the description 'he was killing this child' then the action was wrong and should not have been done.[18]

If an action is describable as the deliberate killing of a child, and if it is wrong deliberately to kill an innocent person such as a child, then this action that has been described is wrongful killing, namely, murder.

What is the relevance of all this to equality and justice? First, by showing that murder is objectively describable and verifiable, we show that certain acts of injustice are objectively describable and verifiable. And that means that justice, on the contrary, requires at the minimum the avoidance of such objectively describable and verifiable actions. The respect for fundamental human equality requires, at least, that innocent human beings are not deliberately killed, and that no human being is killed by another human being acting as a private individual. Even when someone has committed grievous harm, that person's life cannot be taken by another individual, but only by a representative of the state.

These conclusions, although nontrivial, are nonetheless likely to seem incomplete. And rightly so: for although we know what we should never do, we remain unable to say in advance, with regard to any particular situation, what we should do if we are to act in accordance with the virtue of justice. To return to the sports analogy: although we cannot say what a good play will be in an unfolding football (soccer) game, we can say that it will never involve picking up the ball with one's hands. Just so, justice will never involve the deliberate intention to kill an innocent person. Murder, in the human "game," is out of bounds.

Other Acts against Justice, and the Peculiar Case of Property

Fundamental human equality—which is inextricably connected with justice—is manifested in the conclusion that no individual's life may be taken except by the state and then only when the individual has by positive action lost his immunity from deadly harm (an immunity based in the fundamental human good of life). We may wonder how this analysis plays out in other types of wrongful actions, that is, in such other actions as also are out of bounds for humans. Adultery, lying, and perjury are also wrongful acts (like murder, also forbidden in the Ten Commandments); in a longer book, it would have to be shown that they could be described (as murder was above) in terms that are clear and verifiable. Each of them is an attack upon our social existence, a violation of a fundamental community institution.[19] A proper description would show

how these are actions are always and everywhere wrong, and how the reason for their wrongness is that they are unjust: they harm the community in the relations of its members with one another. But for this Guide, such claims must remain only assertions, as we move on.

The institution of private property, by contrast, presents us with distinctive peculiarities. Personal ownership of stuff, whether it be land or handiwork or some more complex thing, did not exist prior to the Fall. In the state of human innocence, there was no need for private property because all the goods of creation naturally served their various purposes, under the divinely-given human dominion (see Gen. 1.28-30). There was property, in order to fulfill God's intent that everyone be provided out of the bounty of creation; but it was not at that time private property. After the Fall, the same divine intent needed the implementation of private property. Fallen people take better care of things when they own them. (Think of the typical mess of the common room in an undergraduate dormitory!) Property ownership thus comes into play as an adaptation of the natural human dominion over creation in order to serve, under fallen conditions, God's continuing purpose to provide for all people.

So property is natural—even though, we should note, its privatization introduces inequalities between persons. As Aquinas says, an agent of the community (but not an individual) may take away property from one who holds it as a result of unjust actions on his part, such as robbery or theft.[20] But what if there has been no robbery or theft: in such cases, may the community also take property for the sake of promoting the community's essential common good? Clearly, any taxation at all is built on the grounds that property (in a broad sense, including money) may be taken from its private owners and appropriated rightly by the community when it is necessary to do so for the community's sake. In such a case it is not necessary to prove any lack of innocence in the property-holder; all there needs to be is a serious community need for that property. Now of course, the community cannot do too much of this appropriation of property, else it undermine the institution of private property itself and bring on greater harm. Yet we should not forget the emergency situation in which, if the urgency is such that individuals cannot await other recourse, they may take the property of others.[21] If you and your children are starving and there is no other food available, you make take from your neighbor's garden and it is not stealing. Rather, the postlapsarian institution of private property is understood to be suspended for the sake of the principle behind it, namely, the provision of the goods needed to maintain life.

We can define theft, then, as an individual taking the property of others, or the community taking the property of individuals without a serious need to redirect that property to the common good. And we can specify how the equality-concerns of justice play out with regard to the goods needed to maintain life. If those goods are needed for common good purposes, the community, but not the individual, may take them, and it is not theft to do so. Unlike the taking of human life by the state, in this case there is no need for the person to have forfeited his immunity from harm by perpetrating some harm against the community. But like the taking of life, the taking of property may not be done by an individual, save in a situation of urgent need when there is no other recourse. And again, as in the case of self-defense, any such individual action should be understood as an extrapolation of the state's role to an emergency situation.

What Is the True Distinction of the Two Kinds of Justice?

It is traditional to distinguish different kinds of justice. Aquinas himself does so, using the terms "commutative" and "distributive." Commutative justice has to do with the relation of individuals to each other. Distributive justice, by contrast, has to do with the apportioning of a good among several claimants. A just distribution, in the classical formulation, occurs when each is given his due. So while commutative justice has to do with how we treat one another, distributive seems to do with how, all together, we are treated by our society and its agents. Josef Pieper also identifies a third form of justice, which is in a sense the reciprocal of distributive justice, namely, what individuals give to society and its agents. He calls this, following some suggestions in Aquinas, "legal" justice.[22]

It is interesting to note that the account of justice up to this point has been able to proceed without distinguishing between the

kinds of justice. It began with the basic point, that the excellence
of justice is a perfection of the will for the sake of human beings
living well together, and that at its core is the fundamental equality
of all human beings. In the subsequent sections above, I developed
this with an eye to the fundamental human inclinations, interpreted
negatively as immunities from harm, the most stringent of which is
the immunity from harm to one's own life. Behind this discussion
is the paradox of the human being as a social individual, as a result
of which neither the common good nor the good of an individual
good can decisively out-trump the other. So it is part of the common
good, and not solely to the advantage of the potential victim, that
murder not be allowed. Similarly, although for brevity's sake the
point was not developed, it is part of the common good that the
state be limited with respect to the procreation and the raising of
children by their parents. And so it goes, for all the elements of the
complex human good.

None of these points has entailed the commonly-asserted
distinction between commutative and distributive justice. Indeed,
the distinction, which is classical, is respectfully observed by
Aquinas, but one might wonder if he thought much of it himself.
His treatment of distributive justice is brief.[23] Yet there is an
important distinction to be made between two kinds of justice, a
distinction not between the individual and the state, but between
the backwards-looking and the forward-looking aspects of this
virtue.

This distinction was drawn a few centuries after Aquinas by
the Dutch theologian (and philosopher and lawyer, and much
else) Hugo Grotius (1583–1645), who thereby made a significant
Christian revision of Aristotle's thought. Grotius identifies the two
parts of justice as "expletive" and "attributive." Expletive justice
corresponds well with the commutative justice of the tradition.
It is justice in its proper sense, he says, and it involves making
right, a sort of provision of restored equality. But the other part
of justice, for Grotius, is attributive, and that is something rather
different than distributive justice. By "attributive" Grotius draws
our attention to the future-orientation embedded in any act of
justice, how it lays the ground for the way people are to be with
one another in the future. Attributive justice is action fitting to the
situation at hand, an addition to what people otherwise have in
order that they may flourish better.[24]

Attributive justice, it will be seen, is not concerned with equality. It cannot be. Oliver O'Donovan takes as an example a state provision of funds to parents who are rearing children. The justification for such provision is that it is fitting to do so; with such state assistance, parents will be able better to rear their children. We might see it, indeed, as a social deference to the human good of procreation, in which of course there is a strong social interest (since all the human goods work together). Yet however we see it, and however we evaluate such a practice, we cannot see it as giving funds to parents because they are more deserving than other potential recipients of public funds (say, scholars writing Guides in Christian ethics). In such allocations to particular people in defined circumstances, those particular people are treated unequally from all other people.[25]

If Grotius is right in this, then the virtue of justice encompasses, besides equality, a future-orientation that entails a discernment of fittingness. That is to say, to have the excellence of justice means not only treating others with regard to the fundamental human equality that all humans share, but also treating them with a care to do what is fitting to the circumstances. That fittingness cannot help but go beyond what is due on account of equality, as it looks to creative action of the sort to which I have referred as playing the human game well. There is so much more to an excellent life than merely avoiding murder, adultery, theft, and lying. Nonetheless, if we are to have an excellent life, we can have nothing to do with any actions that are always and everywhere wrong, for that is the irreducible respect owed to others' fundamental equality.

Thus justice, it turns out, is more complicated than any mathematics even of the vague sort suggested by the word "equality." Like temperance and courage, justice requires a certain creative improvisation on the spot as it must act not only with regard to human equality but also with regard to what is fitting. To do so, justice, again like the affective virtues, will need to be guided by something beyond itself. What it needs is the further virtue of good sense, the fourth and capstone of the cardinal virtues, that excellence of the intellect by which a person can do justice and act with temperance and courage. Good sense is what we must have if we are to get all the moral virtues into play. Yet even good sense will not be the end. Christian ethics will claim that there are, beyond the cardinal virtues, theological ones—faith, hope, and charity—and that these virtues are also needed. Indeed, the strong Christian claim is that the theological virtues, particularly the virtue of charity, not only work with the cardinal virtues but go further to effect a transformation of the cardinal virtues themselves.

The next chapter, therefore, will attempt to complete this account of how to succeed as a human being by turning to good sense and to the theological virtues, with special attention to the excellence of charity.

* * *

Notes for Further Reading

The adventuresome student will profit from an acquaintance with Thomas Aquinas. His *Summa theologiae* (ST), although by sheer heft not to mention minutely-detailed argument can seem overwhelming, was intended nonetheless as an introduction to the subject particularly for Dominicans in training. It is organized into three parts. Part I, broadly, has to do with God and creation. Part II has to do with human beings. Part III has to do with salvation, and thus with matters of Christology, sacraments, and the like. Part II is divided into two parts, which are known as the First Part of the Second Part (thus abbreviated "I-II") and the Second Part of the Second Part ("II-II"). Throughout, the ST is comprised of Questions, each of which is subdivided into Articles. Thus, a typical reference to the ST might be "I-II.1.2," which refers to the First Part of the Second Part, Question 1, Article 2.

So much for scholarly nomenclature. It is enlightening to see how Aquinas organizes his thought about the human being in Part II. He starts with the end, where the reader will find his careful arguments about the human good. Then, for the rest of I-II, Aquinas deals with such matters as actions, habits, vices, law, and grace. The Second Part of the Second Part is mostly concerned with the seven principal virtues, beginning with the theological and working down to temperance. This organizational structure already reveals that Aquinas's understanding of ethics has much more to do with virtues than with law, even though his treatise on law, I-II.90–108, is justly famous on its own. It is also of note that the entire moral discussion begins with Aquinas's consideration of happiness as the true human end.

For an introduction to Aquinas's thought in general, see Brian Davies, *The Thought of Thomas Aquinas* (Oxford: Clarendon Press, 1992). The title of Davies's chapter on Aquinas's ethics is revealing: "How to be Happy" (pp. 227–49). Elsewhere, Davies reports that Herbert McCabe's introductory Oxford course on ethics was called "How to be Happy." See Herbert McCabe, *The Good Life: Ethics and the Pursuit of Happiness* (ed. Brian Davies; London: Continuum, 2007), x. When we deal with Aquinas and ethics, happiness is clearly in the air.

The following volume contains commentary articles on the various sections of both Parts of the Second Part of the ST: Stephen J. Pope ed. *The Ethics of Aquinas* (Washington, D.C.: Georgetown University Press, 2002). In the notes to this Guide there are many citations of Jean Porter's book on Aquinas's importance, *The Recovery of Virtue*; her chapter on justice in this Pope volume is also worth close study.

A helpful textbook is William C. Mattison III, *Introducing Moral Theology: True Happiness and the Virtues* (Grand Rapids, Mich.: Brazos Press, 2008). Mattison's book shows generous sensitivity to the mind and character of American college students.

For another volume on the virtues, by a leading twentieth-century philosopher and theologian, see Josef Pieper, *The Four Cardinal Virtues* (Notre Dame, Ind.: University of Notre Dame Press, 1966).

Turning to war, Michael Walzer's *Just and Unjust Wars* (New York: Basic Books, 4th edn, 2006) is a standard and well-regarded contemporary philosophical treatment.

James Turner Johnson's *Morality and Contemporary Warfare* (New Haven: Yale University Press, 1999) takes "just war tradition" (his preferred formulation, without the definite article, and not "just war theory," for what we have is a tradition of ways of thinking in the midst of conflict as well as around it) and applies it to such contemporary challenges as humanitarian intervention.

Oliver O'Donovan's *The Just War Revisited* (Cambridge: Cambridge University Press, 2003), besides four exceptional essays on Christian thinking about war, has a chapter, "Counter-Insurgency War," that deals with issues of terrorism (see pp. 64–77).

Paul Ramsey was a key figure in the theological recovery of the Christian tradition of thinking about war in the post-World War II era. See his *War and the Christian Conscience: How Shall Modern War Be Conducted Justly?* (Durham, N.C.: Duke University Press, 1961). Ramsey also wrote many occasional articles, some of which are gathered in *The Just War: Force and Political Responsibility* (New York: Charles Scriber's Sons, 1968).

Francisco de Vitoria, a sixteenth-century Dominican (c. 1485–1546), is an important early modern source of Christian thinking about war. His *relectio* "On the Law of War" is contained in the very welcome collection edited by Anthony Pagden and Jeremy Lawrance, *Vitoria: Political Writings* (Cambridge: Cambridge University Press, 1991). From Vitoria's writings come such contemporary *jus in bello* criteria as "discrimination" and "proportionality," as well as a concern for the state of affairs once hostilities cease. Vitoria is worth reading, also, as one of the great commentators on the Second Part of the Second Part of Aquinas's ST. Those writings, alas, are mostly untranslated.

With regard to Christian thinking about property, the student might read what is in all likelihood the most influential of papal encyclicals, Leo XIII's *Rerum novarum* (1891). John Paul II's *Centesimus annus* (1991) purports to be a continuation of Leo's thought into the changed circumstances following the collapse of communist regimes. As regards property (unlike its teaching on the state), it probably is. Encyclicals can be found on the Vatican website, www.vatican.va, in various languages. These particular social encyclicals are also often reprinted in anthologies. Claudia Carlen ed. *The Papal Encyclicals 1878–1903* (Wilmington, N.C.: McGrath, 1981), contains all of Leo XIII's encyclicals, with bibliographies of commentaries upon each. *Rerum novarum* is at pp. 241–61. J. Michael Miller ed. *The Encyclicals of John Paul II* (Huntington, Ind.: Our Sunday Visitor, 1996), contains *Centesimus annus* at pp. 571–650. Miller provides an extensive introduction and select bibliography as well.

The masterful work of Hugo Grotius, *The Rights of War and Peace*, has been newly edited by Richard Tuck and published complete in three volumes in English translation (Indianapolis, Ind.: Liberty Fund, 2005). Vastly shorter, and to the point about attributive justice, is the essay by Oliver O'Donovan, "The Justice of Assignment and Subjective Rights in Grotius," in

Oliver O'Donovan and Joan Lockwood O'Donovan, *Bonds of Imperfection* (Grand Rapids, Mich.: Eerdmans, 2004), 167–203. For a manageable extract from Grotius, see Oliver O'Donovan and Joan Lockwood O'Donovan (eds), *From Irenaeus to Grotius: A Sourcebook in Christian Political Thought* (Grand Rapids, Mich.: Eerdmans, 1999), 787–820. This selection also includes Grotius's thoughts on punishment, one of the few Christian theological reflections on that aspect of justice.

CHAPTER FIVE

Good Sense and Love

Although good sense, the human excellence by which we make good decisions, pulls together all the preceding virtues, it also falls short of complete human happiness, for which we need the theological excellences, particularly love

Jane Austen

Once when teaching seminarians a course in Christian ethics, I included Jane Austen's novel *Emma* on my syllabus. It provoked bemused curiosity, both within the class and outside. What is a work of fiction doing in an ethics class? And why this one?

I put it at the midpoint of the semester so that the students would read *Emma* immediately following our work on the development of the virtues. Their assignment was to read it for enjoyment, while taking notes as they went along on how the various characters, particularly Emma herself, made decisions. In that regard it is a book that produces remarkable and fruitful conversation. For Emma makes a number of colossally bad decisions through the novel. She often thinks she knows exactly what would be best for her various friends and acquaintances, and she wills them to follow her along for great lengths, only to bring them to bad ends. She must realize, at the end of the novel, how most of the conceptions she had formed of others' characters and motives were erroneous. She had failed, at nearly every turn, to have good sense. The book poses, largely by striking counter-example, the question of how to make good decisions.

The phrase "good sense" is attributed by Herbert McCabe to Jane Austen, and he calls it "a nearly perfect English equivalent" for the Latin *prudentia*.[1] That virtue's key element, according to William Mattison, is "seeing." To have good sense, Mattison says, is to see truthfully, to see things as they really are and, without a gap, to act accordingly.[2] Emma often failed to see what was clearly obvious to everyone around her, and failed furthermore to perceive how her own actions would be interpreted by others; and with these failures of sight she thus failed to make good decisions. It is quite a plausible starting-point, to make "seeing" central to good sense.

I have used *Emma* not only in seminary but also in parish book reading groups. It can be relied upon to lead to lively conversations; people have much they want to say about Emma. But never have I heard anyone say this: "Emma should have just followed her conscience." Following your conscience, it turns out, is not the way to develop good sense. But why is that? In order to understand what is meant by exercising good sense, we need to distinguish it from the common language of "just follow your conscience." What is conscience, anyway?

Why Jiminy Cricket Is Wrong about Conscience

In the 1940 Walt Disney film *Pinocchio*, Jiminy Cricket tells the title character, in a song that lives on in the memory banks of baby boomers and in many a YouTube video clip, that he should always let his conscience be his guide. Jiminy Cricket is, in fact, a personification of Pinocchio's conscience, and Pinocchio ignores him to his detriment. It is a charming film with beautiful early animation and catchy, singable tunes. It is also, unfortunately, quite wrong about the matter of conscience.

At least for Aquinas, conscience has only a small role in moral thinking. It is simply me coming to a judgment about behavior that is either in the past or under present consideration. There is nothing esoteric or hidden about conscience; it isn't a mysterious faculty inside us that, if we but consulted it, would tell us what we should do. It's not a voice that whispers in our ear. For Aquinas, according to McCabe, conscience is not a faculty or power which we exercise, nor a disposition of any power, nor an innate moral code, but simply the judgement we may come to on a piece of our behaviour in the light of various rational considerations. Usually it is a judgement we make on our past behaviour, but it can be extended to judgement on behaviour about which we are deliberating. Plainly such judgements happen, and they are important when they do; but what is meant in modern talk by conscience is normally something quite different. Nowadays we speak of someone 'consulting her conscience', rather as one might consult a cookery book or a railway table. Conscience is here seen as a private repository of answers to questions, or perhaps a set of rules of behaviour.[3]

One problem with conceiving of conscience as a hidden faculty that generates pronouncements upon actions, pronouncements that instruct us on what we should do, is that such deliverances of conscience are taken as mandates with which we should not argue. If your conscience tells you to do something, on this view you should simply do it. And if it doesn't seem to *me* that it is the right thing for *you* to do, still I should recognize your right to follow your conscience. I pointed out some logical difficulties with this sort of moral subjectivism in Chapter 1. By contrast, in the view of conscience that Aquinas has, conscience is just a step in the process by which I come to a judgment upon behavior. There is nothing in this view that says that the judgment I come to is necessarily right, or that you shouldn't argue with me about it if you think I'm wrong.

Conscience, in other words, is the name for a part of what good sense involves, specifically, the drawing of a conclusion about a piece of my activity. But good sense involves much more than simply such a conclusion.

Making Judgments

When you are reasoning in mathematics or logic, if you are reasoning correctly your thought-processes will be "truth-preserving." That is to say, given true premises and correct reasoning processes, the conclusion will be true as well. Let's look at a few examples of this sort of reasoning.

"Every even number can be divided by two. Six is an even number. Therefore six can be divided by two." The reasoning process is correct, and the premise is true. So, given the number six, the conclusion is true.

"Every man from New York is dishonest. Victor Austin is from New York. Therefore Victor Austin is dishonest." This reasoning process is correct; in fact, it is the same process as the first example. The premise, however, is not correct, since there is at least one honest man in New York. So we cannot know whether the conclusion is correct or not. Victor Austin might or might not be dishonest.

"Every person who has written an ethics book is brilliant. Claudette is brilliant. Therefore Claudette has written an ethics book." Here the reasoning process is incorrect. So even if the premise were true, and even given that Claudette is truly brilliant, we could not conclude that she had written an ethics book.

Now notice what happens when we add additional information. "Every even number can be divided by two. Six is an even number. Six is the number of beers in a six-pack. Jane Austen wrote six novels. Victor Austin is from New York. Claudette is brilliant. Therefore six can be divided by two." The truth-preserving character of the reasoning is not at all affected by the addition of more information.

That's how we reason about many things. But it is not how we reason about practical matters, when we engage in deliberation about things we are considering doing. Consider these examples.

"I want to be healthy. Running laps in the park helps people be healthy. I shall run laps in the park." This is good enough, as far as it goes. Running laps in the park should help me be healthy, all other things being equal. But are they?

"I want to be healthy. Running laps in the park helps people be healthy. Today the temperature is sweltering and humid. I shall run laps in the park." Is this a good line of deliberation? We now have additional information about the weather, which information suggests there might be problems with the conclusion.

"I want to be healthy. Running laps in the park helps people be healthy. Today the temperature is sweltering and humid. Because of a weakness in my heart, my doctor has cautioned me about exertion in hot and humid weather. I shall run laps in the park." This is clearly a bad line of deliberation. In fact, if the speaker carries out her conclusion, she is likely to accomplish the very opposite of her intent; rather than advancing her health, she may make herself sick.

Instead of preserving the truth of its premises, reasoning about practical matters aims at preserving satisfactoriness. All other things being equal, going for a run is a satisfactory way of meeting the desired good, health. But when additional factors are added, this kind of reasoning needs to attend to the question of whether the conclusion still follows with satisfactoriness.[4]

I have said that good sense is an intellectual virtue. Now we see what its excellence consists in. Good sense involves the ability to identify and properly take into account the information that is relevant to drawing appropriate conclusions for action to achieve the good that is desired. With this virtue, a person "sees" the pertinent facts and also "sees" how they pertain. Again, here are two examples.

Condi wants to get to Washington, D.C., from New York. She knows she could travel by car, bus, train, or airplane. Traveling by car entails the complications of parking, and would prevent her from reading on her trip. Airplane travel is the fastest, but it also involves the hassles of going through security at the airport, and, in New York, of getting out to the airport, which take away most of the time savings. Train travel is attractive, but often more expensive than the other modes. She has a friend who regularly travels to Washington by bus and who has encouraged her to try it, commending a particular bus line for its comfortable coaches, electric outlets at each seat (so she could plug in her computer and work on the way), and that it picks up passengers on West 34th Street, not far from her office. Condi decides to give the bus a try.

This seems to be a sound piece of practical reasoning. One might wonder if Condi has taken more time to reach this decision than it was worth, but (on the other hand) if she might be going to Washington more frequently in the future, she will be glad to have had first-hand experience of the bus. (Furthermore, someone with the developed excellence of good sense will not need to spell out laboriously the steps of her reasoning; she may move directly to good action. Nevertheless, an account could be made of her action that revealed its intrinsic sensibleness.) And even now, Condi needs to be alert to such new information as might require her to reason some more. When, say, the night before she travels she catches a news report about a bus having flipped over (the driver is alleged to have fallen asleep), Condi may decide she should check to see if her bus line is the same as that one; in addition, she may try to find out the safety record of her bus line. Again, there will be the question of whether the time spent gathering information is worth it. Good sense involves the ability to come to a decision within an appropriate time, gathering the information needed and also "seeing" when further information will delay harmfully the action that needs to be taken. In her case, she needs to get to Washington by a certain time, and she may have many other things (besides working out her travel) that she needs to do before traveling.

A second example: Joseph wants to be able to read the commentaries of Francisco de Vitoria on the Second Part of the Second Part of Aquinas's *Summa theologiae*. He has learned from a book called *Christian Ethics: A Guide for the Perplexed* that these commentaries exist, for the most part, only in their original Latin. Joseph doesn't know any Latin. He orders a $19.95 Latin course (two 30-minute cassette tapes) from eBay.

I think we would agree that Joseph fails to show good sense here, much as we would all (!) agree that to read Vitoria on Aquinas is of surpassing intrinsic value. Does Joseph even have a cassette player? What does he think he can learn from two half-hour tapes? Has he ever learned a foreign language? Is he aware that there are many different varieties of Latin—classical, medieval, ecclesiastical, and so forth? We wonder if he is the sort of person who "sees" a lot of things, but lacks the skills to discriminate amongst them. Joseph might be a person of frequently changing intellectual enthusiasms; perhaps yesterday it was bioethics, today it's Vitoria, and tomorrow, what will it be? He can make quick decisions to order relatively inexpensive items on the internet, but is he capable of making a significant decision that will shape his life substantially over a long haul? At least in this example, he fails to demonstrate that he sees what's involved in pursuing the good he would undertake. In that regard, he lacks good sense.

Grasping the Ends of Action

So good sense involves quite a deal more than merely discovering one way to get to the end that you desire; you need to grasp all of the relevant features of a situation, and weigh alternative means to your end, in order to achieve that end. This is more of an art than a deductive science, and something that involves experience and practice—features that belong indeed to virtues. This activity, technically, results in the judgment that is your conscience. Your conscience is you, coming to a decision about the rightness of action in the light of the purposes that you wish to achieve. Good sense requires that one be able to make such judgments of conscience well.

But conscience is only a part of the picture. Before one deliberates about means, one must have a grasp of the end of action. In the examples above, the ends were things like becoming healthy, getting to Washington, and acquiring the ability to read Vitoria in Latin. In such examples, the ends of action are simply given. Where do we get these ends?

They usually come from other things that we already want. He wants to read Latin because he wants to read Vitoria's commentaries, and they exist only in Latin. The desire for the ability to read Latin, an end of action, is itself the means to a further end, namely, reading Vitoria. Or she wants to go to Washington because of a new business opportunity. The end of getting to Washington is the means to some higher end.

Yet sometimes the ends are desirable in their own right, without consideration of their relationship to further ends. Health, for instance, is desirable in its own right. Of course, someone might want to be healthy because healthy people are more attractive. He wants to advance in management, and he thinks he is more likely to succeed in that if he exudes an aura of good health. Nonetheless, he is assuredly missing something if his thinking is strictly instrumental. For health, beyond its personal advantages, is also something good in itself; it doesn't need further justification.

The ability to grasp the good that is the end of action has a technical word: *synderesis.*[5] Its most general formulation is to seek the good and avoid evil. This general principle is something we just grasp and understand, without any further justification. When we see that health is good in its own right, or that murder is evil in its own right, then *synderesis* is in action. And, by extension, whenever anything is seen by us as good or evil, as something for which we should aim or from which we should turn, it is so presented to us by *synderesis*. "The intellectual grasp of the aim as aim (not the attraction to it and intention of it, which is the actualization of will, but the understanding of it) is *synderesis*."[6] So McCabe, who also describes *synderesis* as the "natural dispositional grasp" of the need for our practical reasoning to be satisfactoriness-preserving.[7]

Synderesis is distinguished from intention, in that intention belongs to the will and *synderesis* to the intellect. But this is a fine distinction. I think it helpful at this juncture to remember the three elements of the moral act. (1) A moral act has a good intention, that is, the person doing the act intends to bring about some good or to avoid some evil. (2) A moral act is also the right sort of thing to do. In the last chapter's discussion of murder and other acts of injustice, the point was made that such actions have a narrative description that makes them specifiable in terms that do not require knowledge of the intention of the actor. In particular, it is always wrong for a private individual, except when acting in self-defense, to kill an innocent person. (And the exceptional case of self-defense itself may be understood as an implicit state authorization.) I note that such definitions of actions, while not objective as a simple description of physical behavior (i.e., murder is not the same thing as one person killing another), are nonetheless definitions that do not require the invocation of bad intention. (3) Finally, to be moral, an act must be done under the right circumstances. A well-intentioned act, which is in addition something that it is right to do, could be wrongly done. For instance, it is good to be generous, and giving money to a needy friend is a good sort of thing to do. But if you know your friend is likely to do something bad or harmful with the money, or if you have other pressing obligations (say, your child needs medicine that you would buy with that money), then it would not be a moral act for you to give it to your friend.

We are now able to state more precisely the error into which Jiminy Cricket falls. He makes a positive declaration—always let your conscience be your guide—where Aquinas, more cautiously, makes two negative points. First, Aquinas's view is that we should never act against our conscience. Aquinas's reasoning is that if the will acts against what a person concludes (albeit by erroneous reasoning) to be good action, then the person is willing evil or refusing to will good (as she erroneously perceives things to be evil or good)—which is to say that the person is performing serious damage against her own will. She is pitting her will against her intellect. So don't act against your conscience (against what your reason concludes about practical action). But, to bring out the inherent complexity of the topic, Aquinas immediately goes on to say that it is not always good to act in accordance with your conscience! Aquinas puts forth the example of a man who's erring reason (conscience) tells him he should have sexual intercourse with a woman who is married to someone else. He could only reach this conclusion, Aquinas says, by being ignorant of God's law; and of that law he should not be ignorant. A different moral judgment falls, however, upon a man whose reason (conscience) tells him he should have sexual intercourse with a woman whom he (erroneously) takes to be his wife.[8] In this case, his error changes the act into something that is not properly speaking an act of the will—i.e., it's involuntary.[9]

It is wrong not to know that adultery is wrong (and to act in that ignorance), and it is also wrong not to have sexual intercourse with another person's spouse when that's what your conscience is telling you that you should do. As McCabe puts it, Aquinas holds "the disturbing view that you can be in the position of being wrong if you do not follow your conscience and also being wrong if you do."[10] And such situations are far from uncommon in human experience. Ignorant, badly-informed, or carelessly operating consciences are presenting false goods to people all the time.[11]

Developing Overall Excellence

The virtue of good sense involves the fundamental disposition to seek good and avoid evil; it involves grasping the right ends for action; it involves deliberation that preserves "satisfactoriness" as it considers the means to the ends. Since it requires education and practice, good sense cannot be had by a single individual alone, but must develop in just communities where all the virtues are inculcated, where people's affections are rightly ordered and their wills properly attuned to the fundamental equality of people.

A result of good sense is that it is possible for a sensible account to be made of one's actions. Once again I abstract to sport to show the point. When a footballer demonstrates excellence on the field, a broadcast announcer can explain that in which his excellence consists. The footballer's actions may have been quite unexpected; they may have shown commendable innovation in the intelligent application of his personal skill to the circumstances of the game. But the footballer is not first thinking "I could do X and then Z," he just does X and then Z. The point is that his actions embody an intelligence of which an account can be made.

Just so for any person who has good sense. She need not, as she lives her life, be conscious of the various decisions that go to make up her virtuous/excellent activity. Nothing about the cardinal virtues requires that she be at all times conscious of how they are operative. But even if she does not do so herself, an account of her actions *could* be made, a narrative within which her actions would be intelligible and her excellence manifest in its intellectual structure. In the profoundest sense, what she does *makes sense.*

It is the opposite for someone who lacks good sense. In fact, the very question we might ask about such a person is, "What was he thinking?" There is, often quite blatantly, a disconnect between the aims of such a person and what he actually does. And there may be other disconnects, such as being alternately overly rash and then unnecessarily timid, or being unhealthily abstemious one day and out of control the next. To ask "What was he thinking?" is not to suggest that his problem was intellectual; rather, the question points to the lack of intelligibility in his actions. It is an intellectual problem in that, lacking the intellectual virtue of good sense, his appetites and his will are also ungoverned, not properly coordinated to his succeeding at being human.

One might object at this point to the implicit identification of good sense and a coherent personal narrative in which one is succeeding at being human. Can we not imagine a wicked person whose actions all hang together in a coherent narrative? How about a vicious man who constructs a system of concentration camps? Would he not have the personal affective virtues of temperance and courage, in order to achieve his purposes? Would he not have a version of justice, in which he treated as equal, not all human beings, but a subset of the race? Would he not, also and necessarily, have a virtue of good sense at least to the extent that he was able to act over time in a coherent way in order to fulfill his purposes?[12]

In Chapter 2, when critiquing both narrative and rule-based Christian ethics, I argued that the judgment upon narratives requires something beyond those narratives' self-consistency and richness of texture. Just so, true human flourishing needs more than the cardinal virtues alone: we need a gift that we cannot give ourselves. Nonetheless, there are reasons to expect that a bad narrative will not in the end hang together on its own terms—that it will prove impossible for a vicious man to exhibit the cardinal virtues in a coherent way all contributing to his evil project. For, according to the Christian root understanding, sin is a rupture of right relationships in every dimension. Sin is alienation from God, from other people, and from the created world; it is also a self-alienation.[13] So it could be expected that the lack of good sense would be manifest in self-contradictory behavior in a person, in behavior that does not "hang together"; behavior, in other words, about which we cannot tell a coherent story. And we would expect that the schemes and accomplishments of an inhuman tyrant would collapse, eventually, of some sort of internal contradiction.

Still, the mention of sin rightly introduces a critique of the cardinal virtues. For, thus far, I have analyzed human excellence as something to be worked towards, paying attention to the broad categories in which we need excellence in order to do well as human beings. In order to carry out projects over time, we need to have our affections at a state of excellent operation, which is the point of the excellences of temperance and courage. In order to live well with other human beings, we need our will to be brought to that state of excellence which we call justice, and which is, fundamentally, a regard for the radical equality of other human beings with oneself. And in order to do all of this, we need to make good decisions about what actions will bring about the instantiation of these virtues, which is the point of good sense (or prudence), an excellence of the intellect that provides a sort of internal governance over the moral excellences of temperance, courage, and justice.

The Christian critique is that this picture of the cardinal virtues in their wondrous interrelations and organic unity is not the whole picture of a fully human being. Besides the cardinal excellences, there are three called theological: faith, hope, and charity. (It is perhaps worth noting that the Latin *caritas* is translated both as "charity" and as "love." I will sometimes use either word. Each has its limitations: charity wrongly connotes [only] giving assistance to needy persons, and "love" is so widely used that it probably connotes nothing at all.) In the next section, I will look at each of the theological virtues. Here, I will conclude with a comment again about what the "Christian" is in "Christian ethics."

If Christian ethics says that the cardinal virtues fall short, it does not mean anything less than that the flourishing of every human being requires the theological virtues. For Christian ethics is about what's good for human beings full stop (and not about what's good for some human beings only).

And if the cardinal virtues fall short, then Christian ethics can be expected to supply additional content that clarifies, reinforces, and possibly supplements or corrects what the cardinal virtues would be on their own.[14] Here we should expect, in particular, some clarification of the right ends of action, and consequent re-location of the proper mean of each excellence. In fact, the discussion in both the last chapter and this one has proceeded under a broadly Christian understanding of the human good. This four-fold good, as I have laid it out, is understood as intrinsic to the created human being. It is the good of life, which we humans share with all living things; of reproduction, which we share with animals; of social, linguistic life, which is distinctive of rational beings—and the good of knowing the truth about God, which consummates, let us now say, in friendship with God, or eternal life.

That highest element of the four-fold human good is what the theological virtues help us to achieve. But they also shape the human good of living in society. I will show this, in what follows, particularly with regard to the excellence of charity. It is a conclusion the reader might well expect, that charity/love would be an excellence conducive to human sociality. And to circle back to the beginning of this critique: it is the reality of our self-alienation and social-alienation—the reality of sin—that puts urgency in the need for theological virtues to give shape and content to the virtue of good sense. Without the excellence of love, alas, human societies can seem a rather grim business.[15]

Faith, Hope, and Love

These excellences are called "theological" for three reasons. First, because they have God for their object: a person who has faith, hope, and love is being shaped for personal union with God. Second, because they cannot be acquired by unaided human effort: these excellences are gifts of God that go beyond the primal gift of created nature. And third, because they cannot even be known by unaided human reason: God teaches us about them, principally through the Scriptures and the community formed around them.[16] The Christian claim here is that God desires every human being to be united with him. But that union would be impossible, not only because of sin, but also because, as creatures, human beings cannot love or be loved by God. Hence God has provided means of grace, and told us about those means, so that we can be united with him. In this union is complete human happiness, our full success at being human.

Every sentence of that claim needs to be unpacked. I start with the difference between creator and creature. While we cannot in any way imagine what it means to be a creator, we can understand what a creator is not. First, a creator is not something in the world. No fellow creature in the universe can be the creator of the universe. And the reason for that is simple: if I could point to Being X and say, "Being X is God, the creator, the being that created this universe," you could immediately ask, "But who created Being X?" Anything that is in the universe cannot be the creator of the universe and everything in it. Second, a creator is not somewhere "outside" the universe either—for instance, living in some alternative universe. We must keep reminding ourselves that there can be no picture in which both the creator and the universe appear—that, to say it again, God plus the universe do not make "two."[17] This leads to other quite extraordinary claims about the creator. There cannot be more than one creator, for if there were two, we could ask which created which. But, in another sense, we cannot say there is "one" creator, for the whole notion of counting is based on *kinds of things* of which we can have *various instances*. And the creator is not a kind of thing. You could have two cats, if you wanted to (I'd rather not, thank you very much); you could have two diplomas, two children, two cars, even two husbands.

Cats, diplomas, children, cars, and husbands are kinds of things of which we can have various instances. But you cannot have two creators.

Our point is this: God, the creator, is so extremely odd that we cannot put him and the world together in any sort of framework. In other words, there can be no relationship between God and a human being, other than the completely mysterious one that God gives existence to the human being. The notion of creation, by itself, rules out the possibility of a relationship of love.

And all this, we could figure out by unaided human reason. The Christian revelation that is given to us, however, is that God has done something more than merely give us our existence (our being, our nature). God has made it possible for us to have personal union with him. And he has done so in a way that will not destroy our humanity. Rather (in a fitting yet totally unexpected twist in the human story) our union with God will perfectly fulfill us precisely as human beings, while giving us an end that lies beyond mere creatureliness.

The point of the theological excellences is that they shape the human being for her completion in union with God. Faith, hope, and love, as the theological excellences, make it possible for God and a human being to be friends. This is a surprising and radical transformation of what it means to be a creature.

Let us look at each excellence in turn, starting with faith.[18] Faith properly speaking is not a matter of believing those things that humans can figure out for themselves, such as that God is the creator, the cause of the being of everything that exists. Rather, faith is believing matters of revelation, such as those that are stated in the creeds (Apostles' and Nicene), that God is Father, Son, and Holy Spirit, that the Son became a human being, died, and was raised from the dead, and so forth. Faith thus is propositional; what one believes can be put into words. These propositions lie somewhere between knowledge and opinion. Faith is not true knowledge, in the sense of comprehending something; a person with faith does not understand God the way that a botanist understands a geranium. But nor is it mere opinion, for when we have an opinion about something, we simultaneously hold back and say we might be wrong. Brian Davies compares having faith to trusting a doctor. If your doctor tells you that you have kidney stones, and you put your trust in your doctor, then from that point on you will not have a mere opinion that you have kidney stones. You might even say that you "know" you have kidney stones. It isn't true knowledge in you, but rather something that's analogous to faith.[19]

Faith thus is an excellence of the intellect, while not being merely propositional. In the original Latin and Greek texts, and in most modern translations, the creedal language is to say that I or we "believe in."[20] That is to say, the person who recites the creed is not merely affirming propositions that God is and has done such-and-such; she is confessing that she puts her trust in—believes in—the God who is and has done such-and-such. Thus faith presents itself as a matter of trust and personal disposal. It is a gift of God, as a consequence of which one is drawn towards God. One does not accept the articles of Christian faith (again, for instance, as stated in a creed) because they have been proven to be true, for no such proof is possible. One can show that there is no contradiction between the articles of faith and reason—or at least, given any particular claim of such a contradiction, it is the task of theology to show that the claim of contradiction is unfounded.[21] But one cannot go on to proof of what is believed. So faith remains a divine gift, not a conclusion of an argument.

In the end, faith has about it the character of love, in that a person who has faith is drawn towards the object of her belief. And we can understand this connection. Suppose Mary and John love each other, and each gives evidences to the other of their love. There is nothing in the behavior of either that suggests anything to the contrary. Now suppose Paul comes along and tells Mary that John is unfaithful to her. She cannot deny the abstract possibility that this is true. But apart from Paul's statement, there is no other evidence of infidelity. So she rejects what Paul says, and she continues to have faith in John. Why? At the end of the day, it is because she loves him.[22] Similarly, faith in God involves attraction to God; faith cannot be separated from love.

To turn to the virtue of hope is to turn from an excellence of the intellect (faith) to an excellence of the will. The content of this virtue is hope for eternal life with God. This hope is for oneself, but also reaches out, through love, in hope for others. With the virtue of hope, a person continues faithfully through difficulties and challenges. Like the moral virtues of justice, courage, and temperance, hope is concerned with becoming someone who can achieve tasks that require persistence and continuity over time. In this case, of course, the perspective is ultimately one that goes on to eternity.

The virtue of love also is an excellence of the will, but in a different sense than hope. Hope directs the will to its end—God—as "something attainable," as Aquinas puts it. Love is the direction of the will to that end as "a certain spiritual union, by which the will is, so to speak, transformed into that end."[23]

Aquinas famously describes the excellence of love as "friendship" with God. This is no casual metaphor for him. As the next chapter of this book will be taken up with friendship, here it will suffice to say that friendship with God is possible only because of grace, whereby God has established the possibility of a relationship of love—"a certain spiritual union"—between himself and human beings. Grace refers to God's radical transformation of the creator-creature relationship. Like hope, the excellence of love—this friendship—begins with oneself but then reaches out to others, even as Jesus' summary of the law begins with the command to love God and moves at once to a second command, like unto the first, to love one's neighbor.[24]

The Theological Transformation of the Excellences

Theologians make a distinction between the natural or acquired cardinal virtues, which are understood basically in Aristotelian terms, and what are called "infused" cardinal virtues, virtues that are given by grace. The basic idea that there could even be such a thing as infused cardinal virtues comes about as a result of the existence of the theological virtues, which are themselves "infused" in that they are gifts of grace. The orientation towards union with God, given by the theological virtues, in turn effects a transformation in the cardinal virtues. Several questions at once present themselves. What is the relation between the natural/acquired cardinal virtues and the infused cardinal virtues? Are the first transformed into the second, or are the second a separate group of virtues, somehow laid on top of, or beside, the first? Are they the same virtues? Does the "infusion" of grace simply add a "plus quality" to the natural virtues, or is it a whole new thing?

And if new, do the old, natural virtues remain after the infusion process?

One simple view would be to deny that there are infused cardinal virtues. In this view, there is a simple distinction between nature and grace. Nature refers to what is given to all human beings, who have a natural end of this-worldly happiness, the good of which is given by life, procreation, and living in society. To achieve this happiness, human beings cultivate the cardinal virtues. And then on top of all this is added grace, which gives a supernatural end to the human being, the happiness of beatitude, living with God. This is an additional good on top of the natural human good, and for the achievement of which God has given additional virtues, the theological virtues of faith, hope, and love.

Aquinas, controversially, argued against this view. As he saw it, the theological good of living with God, for the sake of which the theological virtues are infused into the human being, transforms everything about the human being. And so, besides the natural/acquired cardinal virtues, there are also God-given, infused virtues of temperance, courage, justice, and good sense. The infused virtues differ from the acquired ones in a number of ways. We will look at three: their end, their mean, and how they "set" within the human person.

With regard to end, the infused virtues aim at union with God, that friendship which is realized in the excellence of love (and which includes friendship with other people). As Bonnie Kent puts it, "infused moral virtues make people well suited to the life Christians must live because they are Christians: persons belonging to the household of God, with love of God as the highest good, faith in God's word, and hope for the happiness of the afterlife."[25] This explicitly theological end makes a difference to what constitutes the mean for each virtue. So, to take a standard example for infused temperance, we may consider fasting.[26] Fasting—eating less or avoiding certain foods at given times—is a customary Christian practice. To fast on, say, Good Friday, is a temperate practice for a Christian. But a non-Christian who eats her customary, normal, appropriate, and healthy food on that same day is also being temperate. The mean for temperance with regard to food is different for the infused virtue than it was for the natural. And the point of eating temperately is also different: the infused virtue is part of a complex understanding of the goods of creation, the acquisition of joy and thankfulness, and the enjoyment of God.[27]

For the infused virtue of courage, the standard example is martyrdom. Secularly understood, martyrdom for Christian faith makes little sense, although anyone can understand how dying for a cause can advance the cause. As Mill said, self-sacrifice is intelligible if it makes things better for other people. But martyrdom in itself, especially one that seems pointless in that it lacks the prospect of improving things in the world, is unintelligible and likely to be judged a failure with regard to the virtue of courage. That is, if you are dying "needlessly," your action seems more like rashness than the true natural/acquired excellence of courage. On the other hand, the infused virtue of courage, effectuated in martyrdom for Christ, understands itself as being modeled upon Christ's own example, and a participation even now in the joyful union with God that is believed in and hoped for.

For the infused virtue of justice, the transformation is also in motivation. The natural/acquired virtue of justice is a commitment to treat all people fittingly in light of their radical equality. Infused justice understands all human beings to be, potentially, friends of God, and so places their radical equality on a theological ground that is not given in creaturehood alone. In addition, the transformation strengthens the commitment to the norms of justice. For the infused virtue is able to uphold the actual dignity of every human being (and not be susceptible to the siren call that some humans are more equal than others) since it believes, in the teaching of the Catholic Church's Second Vatican Council, that the Son of God, by taking on human flesh, in some way united himself with every human being.[28] Infused justice also encourages spiritual practices, such as turning the other cheek, that can allow justice to emerge out of a situation of long-standing feud in which claim and counter-claim alternate without resolution. Such practices open the way for grace to enter into ordinary human interactions, sometimes with dramatic effect.

Finally, infused prudence is good sense in deliberating about matters that pertain to eternal life. It is involved in the achievement of actions in accordance with the mean with respect to each of the infused moral virtues already mentioned.

Here I should note that each of these infused virtues seems to do with certain matters only, namely, those matters directed at the ultimate human happiness of living as a friend of God. They do not take away the need for human beings to live well together, in a this-worldly sense, for which the natural/acquired cardinal virtues are still needed. And this brings me to the question of how the infused virtues "set" within the human person. With the natural/acquired virtues, a person has them only when they have become something like a second nature. As we saw in the previous chapter, if one has to struggle to act temperately, one is not (yet) temperate, but merely continent. It seems to be different with the infused virtues, since they are gifts and not achievements won from guidance, practice, and so forth. "Habitual action," Aquinas says, "causes acquired virtue," but it only "disposes persons to receive infused virtues" which, once received, can be preserved and augmented by habitual action.[29] One can have the infused virtue of temperance and, with it, practice Christian fasting, without that feeling easy or natural at all. The gift has been given, and received, but it is not yet integrated into one's whole being. Bonnie Kent elaborates Aquinas's view:

> Like Aristotle, Thomas [Aquinas] holds that virtues acquired naturally, through long practice, work to eliminate contrary emotions. In time the agent feels much less troubled by his emotions and comes to find virtuous actions pleasant. Infused moral virtues, Thomas explains, can indeed have such an effect (that they *can* is important), but they might not have it immediately. Christians can continue to feel internal conflict and have difficulty in exercising the virtues given by God. Infused moral virtues nonetheless provide a Christian with the strength to lead a good life (emotionally tumultuous or not) and keep her from feeling distress.[30]

The end to be desired is the same—a congruence of one's desires with one's excellent actions—and yet the role of effort seems different. Natural/acquired virtues require that one practice, but the infused virtues (whatever the mystery of "receiving" them is[31]) are the effects of grace. Thus the human element of participation cannot be determinative to their presence and power.

Let us take stock. We started with natural/acquired excellences, and although from the beginning we considered them in light of the complete human good (including friendship with God), we were able to speak of them progressively. So the affective excellences (courage and temperance) had to do with informing the affections with the will, so that the human being acted in accordance with her true desires. Then we considered the excellence of the will, justice, whereby the individual human being's will is brought into the broader considerations of what is needed for human beings to flourish as social beings. Then followed good sense, whereby an excellence of the intellect informs the three moral virtues so that, in fact, one does achieve human excellence, both from the intellectual and volitional grasp of the good to the instantiation of means to achieve it.

Then we turned to the theological excellences, for to achieve the full human good means to be made capable of friendship with God. This good requires an excellence of the intellect, namely faith, to be grasped and desired. It also requires excellences of the will, to be pursued with consistency and pertinacity (hope) and to be consummately enjoyed (love).

But the grace of God, which works to prepare for union with God, also works throughout the human being, thus bestowing infused virtues that are oriented towards this end and have their own distinctive means. Is this the final picture?

One could argue that it is, but again, Aquinas provokes us to push further. He seems to say[32] that the natural/acquired cardinal virtues are not, by themselves, truly human excellences. They need, in addition to the unity given to them by good sense, also to be further informed by the excellence of love. On this view even to have the this-worldly happiness of the human good of living well together, we need excellences that are transformed by charity. Are these the infused virtues? It would seem not, if the matters that the infused virtues deal with are only those things that pertain to eternal life with God. And yet they are not the natural/acquired virtues on their own. Perhaps it is best to say (as we have already suggested) that the cardinal excellences can be acquired, by training and practice, but for their proper fulfillment as what they are they need something beyond what they are, namely, the excellence of love.

One final implication of this transformation is worthy of note. For Aristotle, the highest human excellence is that of the practical intelligence, as the excellence of good sense is a kind of capstone of the moral person. But when Aquinas brings in the theological transformation of the virtues by infused grace, then the highest human excellence is an excellence not of the intellect but of the will. What is most important turns out to be not what we know (not even what we know practically) but what we do. Action—love—is the last human word.

Spiritual Practices

It remains in this chapter only to point out something both obvious and profound. If the theological excellence of love necessarily informs all the virtues, and if the virtues are the excellences that human beings need to succeed at being human, and if being human is the point of ethics, then there is a close relationship indeed between ethics and spirituality. And that relationship is this: spiritual practices are the means of practicing the theological excellences.

There are, of course, a great variety of spiritual practices, indeed there are different schools, different large patterns of emphasis and orientation. We could think of Blessed Teresa of Calcutta, for instance, who imbued in her Sisters of Charity a devotion to daily mass, adoration of Christ in the sacrament, and imaginative prayerful consideration of the love of Christ. The sisters, then, go into the world to do the work for which they are famous: loving the poorest of the poor, whom they see as Christ in his "distressing disguise." Teresa often spoke of the gospel on five fingers (putting one word on each finger): "You did it to me" (a reference to Jesus' parable of the last judgment, when people are told that whatever they did for the hungry, the sick, the imprisoned, and so forth, they did to Jesus).[33]

In the Sisters of Charity—a large-scale international organization, dedicated to achieving concrete human goods over the long haul—we see how charity, with faith and hope, transforms human sociality (the constant invitation to the unwanted to be received, an instantiation of justice) and calls forth courage (touching the untouchable) and temperance (bringing one's affections into line with this enterprise). The lives of these Sisters show the close relationship of spiritual practices and ethics.

On a different note, we could look at the institution of Christian hospitals, another large-scale human enterprise to meet the needs of the sick, informed by the excellence of love that sees the dignity of each person and seeks to offer healing and comfort. Although such institutions are under pressure in modern society, and in many cases one might judge they have strayed from their initial vision, it is undeniable that they arose, as early as the fourth century, out of the profound interconnection of spiritual practices and ethics.[34]

A great variety of spiritual practices can be seen in individuals. Some folks are drawn to Bible reading, the imaginative "chewing" upon the word, practices of meditation whereby the Scriptures sink deeply into one's soul and can shape the way one sees reality, the narratives that one perceives in one's own life. Others are drawn to the rococo complexity of the high mass. Others want to pray alone in silence, and strive to banish images from their minds as they seek a serene simplicity. Still others want to be immersed in the world, offering prayers and intercessions perhaps even at great length for the many needs they find around them. And some are students, trying to learn better what their faith says and what it then implies.

In all these ways, and many others, Christians give expression to, and seek nourishment for, first of all, their faith. In prayer, in ritual, in silence, in study, in the world, Christians proclaim their belief in God and increase their longing for him. The same spiritual practices, and at the same time, build up hope, reminding us of its ground, and strengthening the will in steadfastness. And all these spiritual practices express love. Whether reading or praying, whether alone or in a crowd, whether lifted in ecstasy or bent down in the humiliation of the lowest of the low, it is love that is the reality. Spiritual practices and ethics are closely related, because the last word is love.

*   *   *

Notes for Further Reading

The adventuresome student might refer to Servais Pinckaers, *The Sources of Christian Ethics* (recommended at the end of an earlier chapter), particularly its chapter 7, "Is St. Thomas's Moral Teaching Christian?" Here Pinckaers probes the question of the relationship of Aristotelean virtue ethics and the theological transformation of the cardinal virtues. He even provides a diagram (p. 179). Pinckaers entire book is an argument that (1) Christian ethics is human ethics, *and at the same time* (2) Christian ethics is evangelical, that is, grounded in the gospel of God's inviting the human creature into divine friendship. According to Pinckaers, we need not choose between those two propositions. Also of interest is Pinckaers's account (outlined at pp. 230–3) of the historical development whereby conscience came to be seen as the central point of ethics, even as happiness, virtue, grace, and the Scriptures were sidelined and a concern for law and the adjudication of difficult "cases of conscience" brought to the center.

Mattison's *Introducing Moral Theology* (also recommended earlier) has chapters on prudence, faith, hope, and charity, as he continues to present the material in a manner sensitive to contemporary American college students. He also has a helpful account of the infused moral virtues in chapter 16, "Grace: The Gift of the Holy Spirit for the Virtuous Life."

On the point of God's causality not being "competitive" with the free human actions that he causes (so that they are at once caused by God and yet free), and for reflections on the implications of this point for debates about grace and merit, see Charles Raith II, "Calvin's Critique of Merit, and Why Aquinas (Mostly) Agrees," *Pro Ecclesia* 20 (2011): 135–66 (141–4, 157–60).

Finally, a spiritual work: on the formative ethic of the Sisters of Charity, see Mother Teresa, *Where There Is Love, There Is God* (ed. Brian Kolodiejchuk; New York: Doubleday, 2010). One could helpfully dip into this book at almost any random point. There are summaries in the introduction and in the maxims and prayers at the end, pp. 353–62.

CHAPTER SIX

Friendship

*The excellence of love really is friendship with God,
which makes it possible for success as a human being—
happiness—to be living in friendship with all God's friends*

Surprise and Suspicion

The ethical interest in friendship has arisen conjointly with the contemporary interest in virtue ethics. Aristotle laid out the path when he put a long exploration of friendship into his *Nicomachean Ethics*, immediately following the virtues,[1] so it is natural in a way for us to turn also to friendship in this Guide. Yet it may surprise the casual reader to find that we do so. One aim of this chapter is to show that friendship rightly has a home in Christian ethics.

When we understand human excellences in terms of the natural, acquired virtues, the goal we find is to live well together in society, and the virtues of good sense and justice, courage and temperance form one complexly integrated human excellence with that in mind. But when Christian ethics understands human excellence in fully theological terms, the goal is to be united with God in eternal life, which is to say to have the excellence of charity, a divine gift infused into a person that complexly integrates all other human excellences. This charity is, according to a brilliant move made by Thomas Aquinas, friendship with God. And so, a second aim of this chapter is to explain what friendship with God is, and how it relates to human friendship.

In the *Nicomachean Ethics*, Aristotle distinguishes three types of friendship, according to what the friendship is based upon;

they are friendships of pleasure, of utility, and of goodness. The first two are not friendships in the fullest sense, although they are nonetheless common. A pleasant friend is someone you like to be around because he pleases you, and the feeling is mutual. The pleasure could be one of touch, or sight, or wit, or something else. The point is that you each like the pleasure you get from the friendship. A useful friend, by contrast, might not be pleasant company, but he has something you need (and, presumably, you also have something he needs). What is valued in that friendship is what you get out of it. Only in the third case is friendship true, when the friendship is based on goodness. Such friendships are certainly useful, in that a good friend will encourage you to be good yourself, and they are pleasant, in that the good is also pleasant (at least in the long run). But the point is the goodness of the friend and the goodness on which the friendship is based, not its pleasure or utility.

With this in the background, there could well be suspicion that friendship can have little place in Christian ethics, because Christian faith calls for a kind of love that is in many respects the direct opposite of friendship. For instance, Christians are supposed to love all people, but friendship is love necessarily focused upon particular individuals, and their number can't be very big. Christians are supposed to love people regardless of what sort of character they have; they are supposed to love even their enemies. But friendship is a love of persons who are good and worthy of love. Christians are supposed to give without regard for what might be returned to them, but friendship is by definition mutual and reciprocal; it doesn't make sense to say that X is a friend of Y but Y is not a friend of X. There seems to be a vast difference between, on the one hand, the ideal of Christian love, and on the other, friendship.

But this suspicion is based on rather abstract conceptions of Christian love. It will be a useful exercise to interrogate the Scriptures to see what they have to say about friendship. First, to do so will provide an example of how the Bible can be used in Christian ethics. But more to the point, if the Scriptures follow our initial Christian suspicion and show friendship in an inferior light, then it will be clear that this Guide has made a wrong turn and we should stop now and go back. On the other hand, if friendship is spoken of positively in the Scriptures, then we will have a basis for revisiting our initial suspicion and seeing how theology might overcome it.

Friendship in the Bible

The Bible does make distinctions among kinds of friendship; on the most basic level, we find two categories, good or true friends, and bad or false ones. In Deut. 13.6 Moses speaks of persons who may come along with temptations to idolatry. The tempter might be a brother, or a child, or a wife, or "your most intimate friend"; no matter who he is, this bad and false friend is not to be spared severe judgment. When Job is afflicted, he tells his interlocutors who have offered him false comfort that they are the sort of people who do many bad things, including selling out orphans and friends (Job 6.27). They are faithless. And in a psalm, the speaker complains, "Even my bosom friend in whom I trusted, who ate of my bread, has lifted the heel against me" (Ps. 41.9). The antique Authorized Version has a lovely phrase here, calling the one who abandons him "mine own familiar friend." The bitterness of the betrayal of a friend who proves himself false is keenly portrayed in the Scriptures.

But there are also good and true friends. In a different place, the Psalmist asks who can dwell in God's house. He answers: one who does no evil to his friend (Ps. 15.3). The message strongly links human friendship and being close to God: a person who is faithful to his human friend can live with God. In the wisdom collected in the book of Proverbs, we also find good and true friends. A real friend loves at all times (Prov. 17.17). Friends are not to be forsaken, and good friendships are to be honored down the generations: "Do not forsake your friend or the friend of your parent" (Prov. 27.10). Wisdom also points to our need to be persons who can learn from and be corrected by our faithful friends. "Well meant are the wounds a friend inflicts, but profuse are the kisses of an enemy" (Prov. 27.6). In short, true friendship is grounded in doing good, is close to God, is faithful and steadfast, and prefers correction to a false kindness.

And in the Bible there is a person who is called—and celebrated and honored as—God's friend: Abraham. This goes beyond even the exalted language with which Moses was spoken of, when Moses was likened unto a friend: "Thus the Lord used to speak to Moses face to face, as one speaks to a friend" (Exod. 33.11). With Abraham, there is no figure or simile; he simply *is* the friend of God. There are three citations. In 2 Chronicles, God is addressed in prayer as one who gave the land "to the descendants of your friend Abraham" (2 Chron. 20.7). In the comforting prophesies of Isaiah, God prefaces some good news by addressing his people as "the offspring of Abraham, my friend" (Isa. 41.8). The epistle of James, one of the latest books of the New Testament, also knows that Abraham "was called the friend of God" (because of his faith, according to this letter; Jas 2.23). So the first person called by God, the man through whom all the families of the earth would find blessing (Gen. 12.3), the father of the chosen people Israel and also the father of all those who believe (so Paul, in Rom. 4.11)—this person is called God's friend. And between a friend and God there is conversation "face to face," a phrase that points to intimacy and the reciprocity of communion between individuals. And there was faith, the loyalty and steadfastness that we expect to find in true friends.

In Jesus' use of the address, "friend," we confront both the horrifying possibility of betrayal, and also the exalting possibility of something hitherto unimagined: that friendship with God could be extended beyond the foundational figures of Abraham and Moses. First, in Matthew's gospel, Jesus shows awareness that others deride him for being "a friend of tax collectors and sinners" (11.19)—which, of course, he was. Then in two parables, Jesus uses the word "friend" as part of the address to someone who is in the wrong.[2] In the parable of the laborers, the man who worked all day and received the same pay as those who worked less finds his want of mercy confronted this way: "Friend, I am doing you no wrong; did you not agree with me for the usual daily wage?" (20.13). And in Matthew's appendage to the parable of the banquet, a man comes in to the wedding celebration but doesn't dress himself properly. He is asked: "Friend, how did you get in here without a wedding robe?" (22.12).

In both of those parables, the climax comes in a question whose first word is "friend." It ought to be a shock to hear that word so used, and one might hope that the hearer proved himself amenable to correction, that he heard the question as a summons to get real, to rise up out of his grudge, to remember that he is or at least should be a friend to the one who is speaking to him. Just so, it is a shock to the reader of Matthew's gospel to find, not as a parable but as part of the story of Jesus' betrayal itself, the same word put in a question that comes at the climax of Jesus' arrest. Judas had arranged it that he would identify Jesus to the authorities by means of a kiss. He comes up to Jesus, soldiers in violent tow, only to hear this question addressed to him: "Friend, why are you here?" (26.50).[3] Those are Jesus' last words to Judas.

Turning to Luke, in one of the parables he recounts friendship turns out to be an impotent thing in comparison to sheer bothersomeness. It's a parable about the importance of persisting in prayer. In it, one person says to his neighbor who has already gone to bed, "Friend, lend me three loaves of bread; for a friend of mine …" (11.5-6), and Jesus comments that he will get the loaves, not out of friendship, but because he is a bother. So that use of "friend" seems to point to a relationship that's rather superficial.

Luke also gives us an example of an ironic friendship. In his account of Jesus' arrest and subsequent interrogations, Luke tells us of Pilate sending Jesus to Herod, who is glad to have the chance to talk with him. It doesn't seem to do Herod much good, but it patched up his friendship with Pilate: "That same day Herod and Pilate became friends with each other" (23.12). We could see this as more than superficial; it is a strong bond. Yet it isn't shown to us as the best of friendships, but rather an ironic result of Jesus' saving work.

Finally in Luke, we have a teaching in which the Jesus-figure says "friend" in an encouraging way to the character who stands for the faithful disciple. Jesus tells those who would learn from him that they should not seek worldly honors; at a banquet, don't presume to sit in the best seats, but take a lowly place. Then the host of the banquet will come to the true disciple and say, "Friend, move up higher" (14.10). This is set forth as being great happiness: to be noticed, to be invited to ascend, but perhaps most of all to be called, truly, a friend of Jesus.

Both Matthew and Luke thus suggest that Jesus' purpose is to make friends. In Matthew, we see this poignantly in those who turn away from this offered friendship. In Luke, Jesus causes friendship even ironically, and quite invitingly molds his disciples to learn his humility and thus become his friend. But it is in John's gospel that friendship with Jesus becomes most explicitly a description of the point of Christian faith.

First, John the Baptist describes himself as Jesus' friend. It is his joy, he says, to be the friend of the bridegroom, and he rejoices in the bridegroom's voice (3.29). This friendship with Jesus is, in turn, a friendship of Jesus' disciples with each other. Significantly, Jesus says this right at the center of the gospel. At the great "sign" that culminates the first half of the gospel—the raising of Lazarus from the dead—Jesus speaks to his disciples of Lazarus as "our friend" (11.11). Then at the end it is finally plainly said. "No one has greater love than this, to lay down one's life for one's friends. You are my friends if you do what I command you. I do not call you servants any longer, because the servant does not know what the master is doing; but I have called you friends, because I have made known to you everything that I have heard from my Father" (15.13-15). These words are spoken at Jesus' last supper, in an intimate room where his close friends are gathered to him.

So the Bible is clear. The model of faithfulness, Abraham, is God's friend. And Jesus' purpose is to form disciples into being true friends. There is some deep Trinitarian theology here; Jesus' friends know everything that Jesus has learned from God his Father (Jn 15.15). In all these ways, friendship has secured its place at the heart of Christianity.

But the suspicions of friendship also derive from things that Christianity teaches about love—that it is to be universal, and without regard for the character of the recipient or the possibility of reciprocity. So the task is still before us. What sort of account of friendship can theology give?

Augustine: Love the Friend in God

Although friendship has posed peculiar problems for theology and has seldom been taken as a central theological topic, nonetheless friendship has received important attention from major theologians through history.[4] I will look particularly at the two towering Western theologians, each of whom made an important contribution to the development of thought on friendship.

Augustine, in the fifth century, makes love a central theme of theology. In Augustine's doctrine of God, love is the key to understanding the Trinity: the Father loves the Son, the Son receives and returns this love to the Father, and the Holy Spirit simply is that love. He also makes the contrast between two loves the interpretive key to all human history: there is the city of God, which is grounded on love of God to the contempt of self, and the city of man, which is grounded on love of self to the contempt of God.[5] And most personally, Augustine put the love for God at the center of his theological anthropology. Each human person is made to love God, a love that animates everything we do and that can be satisfied, only, by God himself. Perhaps the most-read book, ever, apart from the Bible, is the *Confessions* of Saint Augustine, a book which he wrote in the year 397, in which he confesses love for God as he gives an account of his life up through his conversion and baptism (at Easter in 387, when he was thirty-two years old). The opening words of the *Confessions* are praise of God, and a wonderment whether God can rightly be praised by any human being—for how can we know God without praising him? Yet how can we praise him rightly without knowing him? The first paragraph ends with the famous words that serve, as it were, as the motif of Augustine's life (and that of many others who will find him, in the *Confessions*, as a type of themselves): "our hearts are restless until they rest in thee."

So love is central to Augustine's theology. Friendship, we may also say, was central to his personality. Throughout the three decades that he wandered before his heart could rest in God, Augustine had several friendships. Indeed, after he became a Christian he insisted on living in community with friends, and as a bishop in northern Africa he drew other clergy around him to live a form of monastic life at the cathedral. He seems to have been naturally and culturally gregarious; he valued and cultivated friendships all his life.

Joseph Lienhard identifies Augustine as the first theologian to have a theology of friendship. It appears in the *Confessions*, and continues then to the end of his life. Rather than a relationship based on sympathy, Augustine says that true friendship is a bond that is established by the Holy Spirit, a gift of God's grace.[6] This leads Augustine to a judgment upon his pre-Christian friendships that is at times severe. He reflects at length upon a particular friendship from his youth (or young adulthood) in Book IV of the *Confessions*. He and his friend shared at the time a disapproval of orthodox Christianity, and neither of them had been baptized.[7] His friend took ill and it was thought he might die; while he was more or less unconscious in his fever his parents arranged for his baptism. When he recovered, Augustine visited him and started to mock the baptism as a meaningless ceremony, but his friend rebuked him strongly. Augustine held his tongue, thinking that he would later find his friend in a more pliant mood, when suddenly his friend died. And this was devastating. Some of the most beautifully poignant sentences ever written about human loss are these:

> Everything on which I set my gaze was death. My home town became a torture to me; my father's house a strange world of unhappiness; all that I had shared with him [my friend] was without him transformed into a cruel torment. My eyes looked for him everywhere, and he was not there. I hated everything because they did not have him, nor could they now tell me 'look, he is on the way', as used to be the case when he was alive and absent from me. I had become to myself a vast problem.[8]

The *Confessions* is not Augustine's autobiography, but set out as a prayerful remembering of his past.[9] The middle-aged Augustine, now a bishop, after several further anguished paragraphs of remembering and trying to understand his grief, at the end identifies as his problem that he had loved his friend as if his friend would never die. He should instead, he now says, have loved God that way. He had bestowed his love on the wrong person. With love of God—who will never die, and thus is a sound recipient for human love—Augustine could have loved his friend "in God."[10] And this is Augustine's basic view of friendship. We need first to love God, and then to love our friends in God, who in fact gives our friends to us.

This provides a secure place for human friendship, but at the cost of relegating friendship to a second level. For the love for God, in Augustine's view, seems to be unidirectional, unlike the love of friends. And yet to love a friend "in God" might result in its own unidirectionality, a love toward the friend, a love that promotes the good of the friend, and so forth, without being a reciprocal love which also receives from the friend. Augustine seems to be setting up defenses against the fickleness and weaknesses—the ongoing sinfulness—of actual friends, and against the chances of disease and war. But more fundamentally, says Liz Carmichael,

> Augustine's formal doctrine of love subsumes human friendship within the ordered love that effectively draws all our powers into a strongly one-way love for God. Good so far as it goes, this is not yet an adequate account of our love-relationship with God as known in Christ. Nor does it do justice to love of neighbour.... . [I]t will be little surprise if loving God through the neighbour, or even effectively bypassing the neighbour, will tend to eclipse loving our neighbour or friend in God, let alone with or from God.[11]

For a theological grounding of the reciprocity of love, I turn to the second towering Western theologian, who equates love of God with friendship.

Aquinas: Love Is Friendship with God

I have said that Thomas Aquinas made a brilliant move when he declared that charity simply is friendship with God.[12] Carmichael calls him the "greatest theoretician" of friendship, who uniquely defined "Christian love, *caritas*, fully and in every respect as friendship, *amicitia*."[13] But how can it be that Christian love is the same thing as friendship with God? Aquinas's thought is nuanced and subtle, involving many fine distinctions that this Guide, unfortunately, must pass over. Here is what seems to me to be the skeletal structure of his thinking on friendship, arranged in terms of the principal suspicions or objections to which it responds.[14]

To the objection that Christian love is extended to all people, but friendship involves mutuality, Aquinas says that when we love a friend we love everything about him. Our love will naturally extend to the friends of our friend, even if those friends have no other connection to us. "[W]hen a man has friendship for a certain person, for his sake he loves all belonging to him, be they children, servants, or connected with him in any way. Indeed, so much do we love our friends, that for their sake we love all who belong to them, even if they hurt or hate us."[15] So when we love God, we also love those whom God loves. Each human being is, potentially, a friend of God. So whenever one human being, a friend of God, is loving God, that love is naturally extended to all the other friends of God, that is, to all other people insofar as they are also friends or potential friends of God.

Then there is the objection that friendship, since it necessarily involves sharing because friends do things together and share each other's lives, cannot be the same thing as love of God, since human beings cannot have anything like a common life with God. This objection is based on the radical difference between God as creator and human beings as creatures. To this Aquinas answers that charity/love is God's gift, something that comes to us by grace, and once it has been given, then there is indeed some sort of transformation so that human beings can have communion with—share with, communicate with, have a sort of common life with—God. There's an old adage, "If it's actual, it's possible." Aquinas's point is that, although we cannot understand it, God has actually given the grace that makes it possible for us to have mutuality with him in love, a mutuality that is properly called friendship. "Charity signifies not only the love of God but also a certain friendship with Him ... a certain mutual return of love, together with mutual communion... . Now this fellowship of man with God, which consists in a certain familiar intercourse with Him, is begun here, in this life, by grace, but will be perfected in the future life, by glory."[16]

The previous objection can be formulated also with regard to other people. If friendship involves sharing one another's life, then it cannot be extended to a large number of people, since we are finite beings and cannot have a huge number of friends. But this seems to contradict Christian charity, which is to be extended to all people. Aquinas answers that Christians really will want to communicate with all of God's friends, but they are not required to do specific acts towards every person, because it is impossible to do so.[17] And he gives some concrete advice, which we can connect back to the fundamental four-fold human good. There is a proper friendship with oneself, whereby one seeks preservation particularly of one's spiritual goodness, but also, in its proper place, of one's body.[18] There is also a proper preference given to love of one's family. And there is a proper preference given to one's fellow citizens. One also should love (and will want to love) those who are close to God, those who are more fully realized as God's friends. How one sorts out these differing loves in concrete situations is a task for the virtue of good sense (now itself informed by the virtue of love). Apart from the acts of injustice that are always wrong and which, thus, are always to be avoided, there are not hard-and-fast rules here. Nonetheless, it is signally important that one is disposed and ready to love *all* those that God loves, that one wants to be friends with God and with *all* of God's friends. This desire points, as I will say below, to an eschatological transformation of the possibilities of friendship.

Similarly to the last objection, it could be said that true friendship is based, as Aristotle said, on the good, and thus it is improper to extend friendship to people who are not good—to vicious characters, to people who despise the good. But Christian love is supposed to be directed to all people, especially in a way to sinners and to one's enemies. Aquinas's answer builds on the scriptural ground that God has offered his friendship to sinners and to his enemies. As we noted above, Jesus was called a friend of sinners (Mt. 11.19), and he asked that his own death not be held against those who accomplished it (Lk. 23.34). We can make a distinction between what's offered and what's received. The offer of grace in Christ is universal (Jn 3.16, for instance: "God so loved the world … that everyone who believes … may have eternal life"). The reception of the offer of grace remains in the realm of human freedom, although, again, we cannot understand how such an offer could actually be rejected—just as we cannot understand any particular sin. (As I have said earlier, with sin, we always reach a point in our understanding of it where we are just baffled. "What was he thinking?" we say—and there is at the end of the day no answer, just a void.) Specifically with regard to our enemies, Aquinas says we do not need to make particular actions of love toward them; however, we do need to be ready to love them and to offer them friendship "if the necessity were to occur" (presumably, by their sincere petitioning for reconciliation). Beyond that, he says, it does belong to the perfection of charity actually to love one's enemies, i.e., with particular actions, apart from any necessity.[19]

So friendship with God is, first, the grace given by God loving a human being. This grace makes possible a love for and with God. This is rightly called friendship, since love involves mutuality, communication, and benevolence. Friendship with God necessarily

extends from God to all of God's friends, which is to say, potentially, to all people. It also reveals a transformation of the notion
of friendship, in that, for a Christian person, friendship's longing is
now universal, like God's. It extends not only to the virtuous but
also to the wicked, not insofar as they are wicked, but insofar as
they are loved by God. And it extends, potentially, to all people,
but (in a manner yet to be discussed) without lessening its intimacy
or intensity. That is, the universal intent of Christian friendship
does not militate against the particularity and the richness of it.

As far as I know, Aquinas does not put that last point in
quite those terms. And indeed it is hard to see how the reach of
friendship can be extended without the actuality of the friendship
being watered down.[20] Yet it is a necessary consequence of our
taking seriously that charity is friendship with God. And it means
that our final human destiny—heaven, if you will—can be fully
described as living together as friends.[21]

Heaven: The Place of Friends

A person with the virtue of Christian faith asserts, as a truth of
the Apostles' Creed, that there is a "resurrection of the body."
The point of this claim is to affirm human integrity: that we are
not spirits that happen to have bodies, but unities composed of
body and soul together. Aquinas writes in his commentary on
1 Corinthians: "The union of body and soul is certainly a natural
one, and any separation of soul from body goes against its nature
and is imposed on it. So if soul is deprived of body it will exist
imperfectly as long as that situation lasts…. [S]oul is not the whole
human being, only part of one: my soul is not me."[22] Indeed, it is
because of the unity of body and soul that we are to love our bodies.
In the resurrection, St. Paul writes, we are to be full humans, and
that means we are to be, again, body-soul unities, now with bodies
that are spirit-run (translations of 1 Cor. 15.44 that say "spiritual
body" are misleading: the contrast is between a body, such as we
have now, that is run by its soul, and a body that is run by God's
Spirit).[23] What this means in particular terms is clearly beyond our
ability to comprehend. But there is one thing that it seems to me it
must mean. The spirit-run body of the world to come will be able

to have communion with every other such body. Without ceasing to be human—without, in particular, ceasing to be body-soul unities—we will be able to have friendship in act with every other human being.

Heaven then just is friends living together. Assuredly, the removal of sin will be a great liberation for the possibilities of human action. For sin is negation and subtraction, the spiritual equivalent of unnecessary friction. In physics, when a machine minimizes friction it is running at maximum efficiency. In the case of human beings, when sin is diminished creativity and love are increased. Without mutual animosity, the members of an orchestra work together better. When people share in open communications, without the fear of being betrayed or cheated, they are better able to collaborate and bring about exciting advances in what humans do together. We are fulfilled as persons when we live in free societies: not the free society of the minimalist state, in which sinners continue to exist, but a free society without sin, wherein government exists not to provide police and military, and not to provide courts to adjudicate wrong, but rather to guide its citizens to their fulfillment as excellent beings. And this government, which is the rule of Christ, does so by the gift of grace, the excellence of charity, the friendship with God that is, in the end, the friendship of people living together.

Is this vision of heaven a disjunction from our present reality, or a transformation with an underlying continuity? That is to say, is this vision of human happiness something different from the flourishing of human beings in our present world? Clearly, the removal of sin is a sharp difference from our present circumstances, and so in that sense the vision is disjunctive. And yet, despite that great difference, the human goal remains the same. The human goal is, as it always has been, to have fulfillment in our being, which means, as human beings, to live well together.

This Guide has now touched on heaven, but it has not reached its end. A question remains for the final chapter, the question that will require us to ask what a person is. I will get at that question by confronting the reality of disability. Has this Guide been assuming that a real human being is a fully-abled human being? If so, then all our talk about excellences seems likely to be merely fanciful. But if not, what really is an excellent, fulfilled human being?

* * *

Notes for Further Reading

A convenient anthology of Western philosophical writings on friendship is Michael Pakaluk's *Other Selves: Philosophers on Friendship* (Indianapolis, Ind.: Hackett, 1991). The volume is of modest length and contains helpful introductory essays for each author, plus an overall introduction that situates the recent revival of interest in virtue and friendship in philosophical discussion.

The *Confessions* of Saint Augustine is available in several translations; a competent contemporary one at a decent price with helpful footnotes is Henry Chadwick's: Saint Augustine, *Confessions* (Oxford: Oxford University Press, 1991). Augustine's Latin is classically beautiful; the student who would like to look at it could check out the Loeb edition, in two volumes, with an elegantly antique facing English translation: *St. Augustine's Confessions* (2 vols; trans. William Watts; Loeb Classical Library; Cambridge, Mass.: Harvard University Press, 1912). For background on Augustine, see Gerald Bonner, *St. Augustine of Hippo: Life and Controversies* (Norwich: Canterbury Press, rev. edn, 1986).

A serious study (it is a revised dissertation) is Daniel Schwartz, *Aquinas on Friendship* (Oxford: Clarendon Press, 2007). Schwartz is particularly interested in what Aquinas says about human friendships. He finds Aquinas has an expansive view of human friendship, consistently pushing the concept to wider application. So, for instance, Aquinas finds space within friendship for dissension and disagreement, and space within the concept for a wide variety of friendships; he also accommodates the need for justice and law within friendship.

For theological works on friendship, the best historical study I know is Liz Carmichael's *Friendship: Interpreting Christian Love* (London: T & T Clark, 2004). A perceptive book-length essay that approaches the question thematically is Gilbert C. Meilaender, *Friendship: A Study in Theological Ethics* (Notre Dame, Ind.: University of Notre Dame Press, 1981). Paul J. Wadell has published several books on friendship; one might well start with his first, *Friendship and the Moral Life* (Notre Dame, Ind.: University of Notre Dame Press, 1989).

John Henry Newman has a sermon that nicely works out from the fact that Jesus, whose mission was to call friends, had one particular friend who was closer than the others, the "beloved disciple," John (see, e.g., Jn 13.23). From this, Newman derives practical advice on focusing our love, initially, on the particular persons who are near to us, rather than having a vapid love of everyone (which is often a mask over a particular hate for those close to us). John Henry Newman, *Parochial and Plain Sermons* (San Francisco: Ignatius Press, 1987), 257–63. This is vol. 2, sermon 5, on the feast of St. John the Evangelist.

CHAPTER SEVEN

Disability and Persons

The sense in which there are not gradations of being human, and how the word "person" illuminates this conclusion surprisingly

Kinds of Disabilities, and the Questions They Raise

If Christian ethics is about the flourishing of human beings as such, what is to be said about the flourishing of disabled[1] human beings? Can they flourish only if their disability is removed? That is to say, must a disabled person become a post-disabled person before he can be successful as a human being?

There was a blunt pagan answer, broadly speaking, as we might infer from Aristotle. Human beings whose bodies were imperfect or whose minds were incapable of full rational thought were, to that extent, cut off from the possibility of happiness. For happiness is activity in accordance with human excellence, and human excellence requires a sound body and a sound mind. Correspondingly, the pagan worldview was tragic. Disease or mutilation in war or other calamity could come upon anyone at any time; there was no secure happiness in the pagan world.

Christianity, by contrast, held out the possibility of happiness to all people, regardless of their physical condition or mental capacity. Jesus famously healed all sorts of sickness and cured people of forces that enslaved their minds and souls.[2] In so doing, he restored people to a place in the human community and gave them the capacity to act in accordance with human excellence. He gave them the possibility of happiness.

What is distinctive of the Christian view is its larger notion of happiness—namely, that it includes friendship with God—along with an expansive optimism concerning those who may partake of happiness. Because of the healing power of Jesus, every person is potentially successful as a human being, flourishing and participating actively in the true human goods including divine friendship. The implication of this view is that the disabled will be healed before they enter into their flourishing state.

We may take as exemplary the dramatic healing of the paralytic (Mk 2:1-12). He is carried to Jesus by his friends, but when they find Jesus at home there is such a crowd that they cannot get to Jesus. So they climb to the roof, dig through it, and then lower through the roof the paralytic on his mat. That gets everyone's attention. Jesus heals him and says two things that he claims are equivalent: "your sins are forgiven" and "Stand up and take your mat and walk." This is controversial in the story, as the claim to forgive sins is recognized as a claim of divine authority on Jesus' part. For us, the sticking point is more likely to be the implied relation of disability and sin. If, however, we recognize that there can be sin that afflicts us for which we are not strictly responsible, then we might acknowledge a parallelism. Sin is what divides human beings and turns them against one another. Similarly, disability separates a person from others. What then does Jesus' authority accomplish? Taking away this man's disability, it restores him to a participatory role in human community. Before his healing, he was outside the "crowd," the gathering of humanity that Jesus was drawing to himself. Once healed, he can stand and walk "before all of them."

Acts of healing, thus, are political acts in which human characters are liberated into the possibilities of human flourishing. What then shall we say when the disabled are not healed? The dangerous move is to give up on the eschatological vision—that is to say, instead of speaking of humans teleologically (as potential friends of God), to speak of them simply in terms of the human characteristics they possess right now. This move is rightly called dangerous, for it leads to the denial that disabled persons (and others) are persons in the full sense. That is to say, it posits an implicit gradation amongst human beings, that some have more of the characteristics that make us human than others—that some are more truly human while others are not. History confirms the danger of this line of thought. If some so-called humans are fairly low on the human scale, then it has been thought that things would be better for all if the low-level humans were eliminated. Candidates for elimination have included (and note the dehumanizing work performed by the adjectives): dirty Jews, parasitical aristocrats, blood-sucking capitalists, unwanted children, mental defectives, and those whose lives are deemed not worth living.

Christians need not follow this path away from eschatology. Above, in Chapter 4, being human was set forth as a goal and not a given. Thus while any human being is good (for existence is good in itself), there is also a meaningful sense of speaking of a good human being as one who actively shows the excellences of being human. It was in this context that I introduced Aquinas's notion of the four-fold human good. Does this view in itself amount to a dangerous discrimination amongst human beings, so that those who are significantly less virtuous (less excellent as human beings) might be treated inhumanely? It need not, so long as the eschatological horizon remains. For, also according to this view, every human being is potentially excellent, particularly and especially in the sense that every human being potentially partakes of the grace of charity, i.e., friendship with God.

So at their best, Christians have determinedly resisted acquiescence in efforts to identify sub-human human beings. This resistance has as its solid ground the possibility that friendship with God is a concrete offer made to every human being.[3] But Christians also, at their best, have resisted truncating the human good to a life beyond the grave. Human fulfillment, in the Christian view, is not pie-in-the-sky-after-you-die. For the human good involves excellent activity—happiness—in this life as well as the next. The eschatological horizon prevents Christians from seeing human happiness as either entirely future or entirely present. How do we hold all this together, particularly when we consider those humans who are seriously impaired in their ability to function excellently, to acquire and perfect the virtues? (The issue, however, is not unique to the disabled, as we will see.)

We may put the paradox this way. On the one hand, disabled people are claimed to be human just like the rest of us; no gradations are permitted here. On the other hand, the understanding of what it is to be human, and of the good of the human being, is such that disabled people fall short. In the case of some disabilities, they fall exceedingly far short.

What is to be done? The comparably easier step is in the consideration of physical disabilities. Disability theorists of recent times have argued that disability is a social construct. And to an extent they have a point. If, to take a very simple example, building entrances did not have stairs, then the physical inability to climb stairs would not divide humanity into the two groups of the able-bodied (who can enter buildings) and the disabled (who cannot). Society, in other words, can be reconstructed to mitigate and remove barriers of access, so that people with physical disabilities can participate in their communities just as fully as anyone else.

I cannot see any reason for Christians to withhold a hearty endorsement of such efforts. Provided that the language of social construction does not somehow deny the reality of the physical world, which is first of all not our construction but a divine gift, there is no reason not to do everything we can reasonably do in order to make possible the community participation of persons with all manner of physical limitations.

And there is a further point. The human being is remarkably adaptive. Sometimes that which appears to be a disability is in fact an opening to an unexplored human excellence. One case in point is deafness. Sign language apparently develops organically within communities of deaf people, and as such contains everything that we expect to find in a spoken language: verb tenses, grammatical moods, the alternative-creating possibility of negation, and so forth. (It was attentiveness to this fact that led the beloved eighteenth-century Abbé Charles-Michel de l'Épée to advocate the baptism of the deaf children of Paris.) That is to say, sign language is not a mere transliteration of a spoken language into hand signals; it is, on its own, a true language, one that *uniquely* uses the four dimensions of space and time together. For human beings not to have developed sign language would have been as much of a deprivation as if we hadn't developed Chinese or English.[4]

Hence, not only does it seem possible to open channels of mutual access for all people to join in communities inclusive of the physically disabled, it is also the case that physical disabilities open up new vistas of human excellence. This is because the disability sometimes turns out to be, in its own right, an occasion for an excellence to develop that otherwise could not have done so.

The problem is more complicated when we turn to mental disabilities, particularly those of the profounder sort. Hans Reinders has noticed that often, in the field of disability studies, physical disability is taken as the implicit paradigm for the entire field. Consequently, since for physical disabilities the provision of access and inclusion is the needful path, such is simply assumed to be true for all disabilities. Yet while it is the case that some mental disabilities can be addressed in this way, the severer forms cannot. For a person with profound mental disability simply cannot act autonomously as a willing, purposeful agent. Is then such a person really human? Reinders, who may I say is about the gentlest theologian I have ever met, notes a devastating fact about "our moral culture. Human being does not count as truly 'human' unless it can do something." He introduces us to "Kelly," a twelve-year-old girl in a home he visited. Kelly is micro-encephalic. Thanks to her tiny brain, she, as far as we can tell, has no "interior space." "Kelly never had, and never will have, a sense of herself as a human being." She is entirely dependent on others for those important human activities of "health, safety, relationships, communication, and so on... . Words such as 'I,' 'me,' or 'myself' will never mean anything to her, nor will any other word for that matter." What then can Kelly do? Perhaps nothing more than sigh; perhaps not even that. Nonetheless, the people in the home—remarkably—treat her just like anyone else, e.g., as someone who could be happy or sad; for them, Kelly is just Kelly.[5]

So Kelly is treated as a human by those who live with her, although she would be throughout her life unable to do any of the things that, in this Guide, have been argued to be the substance of human flourishing. Are those who live with Kelly and so treat her simply deluded? Reinders says that the aims of the disability-rights movement are of no benefit to her, for, in her case, access means nothing. And virtue ethics is faced with a deep problem in her, for, in her case, there seem to be none of those basic faculties whose development and strengthening are the means to human excellence and thus happiness. I put it baldly: if happiness is an activity of the whole person over time exercising excellence, what can it possibly mean for a person who lacks any sense of self and cannot sustain activity on her own? Must we, in Kelly's case, put her happiness entirely in the afterlife—if anywhere?

A Brief Look at Contentious Issues like Abortion

This Guide has been probing the perplexities of Christian ethics, a broad subject which, I have tried to show, is not well-understood from the position of particular cases or situations, but needs rather the extended perspective of narratives (including Scripture), character, goods, and virtues. And so the argument has generally avoided contentious issues. But when we consider profound mental disability, we are at the threshold of a host of complex issues that we cannot pass by in silence. All these issues have in common a perception that there are humans who fall short of being fully human in fundamentally significant ways.

The practice of abortion is justified, often, on the grounds that, while abortion is regrettable, it does not terminate a fully human life. Whatever language is used to name the being (embryo, fetus, unborn human), it is taken to be not yet fully human, and therefore something that can be terminated (or killed) on grounds that would be insufficient to justify the killing of a human being. One principal difference here is that, while human beings may not be killed by private individuals but only by agents of the state and only in circumstances where they have committed a grievous harm against the community, the embryo, fetus, or unborn human may be terminated by a private individual and does not need to have committed any wrong against the community.

Similarly, newborn children need not be recognized as fully human. Some modern authors have suggested that killing a child within a certain temporal interval following birth would not be the same as murder (and thus, like abortion, would not fall under murder's restrictions). In a 1972 article, "Abortion and Infanticide," Michael Tooley argues that one is not a person unless one is capable of regarding oneself as the ongoing subject of experiences. Thus it is that not only are some humans (including fetuses and infants) not persons, there are doubtless, he says, some animals that *are* persons.[6] We can go back further. Infanticide was not unknown to ancient Rome, where a child was not admitted to the human community without the permission of the *pater-familias*; lacking that, he or she would be left, exposed, abandoned to die.[7]

At the other end of life, a person in a coma, or a victim of severe brain injury, or a person at the wrap-up of a terminal illness, or someone in "locked-in syndrome"—any such person might in certain circumstances be described as "only a vegetable." The label "persistent vegetative state" (PVS) just in itself testifies to the felt need to make distinctions among degrees of humanity. Someone in PVS, someone who is "only a vegetable," is someone from whom we may withhold food and water, for instance, whereas to do so for someone who is fully human would be deliberately to starve a fellow human.[8]

Now to support the withdrawal of food and water from a person in PVS is not the same thing as to support abortion, and to support abortion in the early weeks is not to support abortion in the later months, and to support abortion at all is not to support infanticide. These are distinct practices. And there are, it seems to me, serious but distinct arguments in support of each of them. And their proponents are not *ipso facto* wicked persons.[9] But what we need to see is that all of these practices involve distinguishing amongst human beings and declaring that some are insufficiently human to warrant the protections and respect that the rest of us enjoy. Those Christians who believe that the human good is an offer for every human being will rest more easily when they can avoid making such distinctions. But is it possible to do so?

The Problematic Word "Person"

The difficulty is that certain distinctions amongst human beings force themselves upon us, so that—whether it is a case of severe mental disability, or merely embryonic existence, or a damaged and likely dying person whose mental capacities have been largely destroyed—we find it hard to see how such humans can flourish, how they can succeed as human beings, that is, how they might participate in the human good and be happy. (The fact that for embryos and infants we are able to ignore this question by focusing on their likely future, in which they will have the possibility of flourishing, does not alter their present reality as humans-incapable-of-flourishing.) Whether we draw from these distinctions any permissions to treat such humans differently from the rest—whether we would permit, say, abortion or euthanasia, or not—it remains the case that even if we would treat them the same we feel the lack of a ground for doing so.

In common parlance, it is often said of such a being that although he is a human, he is not a person, at least not a person in the full sense. This rhetorical strategy, however, is of no initial help, in that it simply shifts the terminology of division. Instead of saying there are some human beings who are lower on the human scale, it says that there are some human beings who are lower on the personhood scale.

Yet the word "person" is in fact quite helpful here, not because it allows a distinction amongst humans, but for the insight it can give into what it means to be a human. There is something different about being human from all other sorts of finite being. And the word "person" is often used to point to that distinctive human difference. To develop this point will require an excursion into trinitarian theology, the Christian claim that God, while one in being, is the three Persons of Father, Son, and Holy Spirit. This excursion, however, will be no mere detour: sooner or later, every Christian discourse must turn to the Trinity. It should not surprise us to find we cannot study Christian ethics without the Trinity turning up.

Let us start with two observations about ancient usage.[10] *Persona* is an old Latin word, meaning roughly a "role" played in the theater; the word can also mean "mask," as it was the case that actors wore masks to identify which role they were playing. Although the etymology is suspect, one may see in the word something like "sounding-through": *per* for "through," and *sona*, from *sonare*, "to sound."[11] The second ancient use was grammatical. Ancient grammarians used "person" to distinguish the three relationships implicit in an act of speech: the one who speaks, the one spoken to, and the one spoken about are in grammar, respectively, the first, the second, and the third person.[12]

In neither of these ancient usages (neither as a role nor as a relationship) is "person" a classifying term. It does not refer to a nature or essence, nor does it refer to a property. For instance, "person" is not a nature that stands alongside "kangaroo-ness" and "cockroach-ness" and "chair-ness" and whatever other things might be essences. Counting up the items in a room, we would not say we had three cats, 250 books, five chairs, four people, and (in addition) some persons. Now we might naturally say that we had four persons, but that would be to use "persons" interchangeably with "people," which is fine as far as it goes (since, I would say, every human being is a person), but the ancient usages about "person" point to something other than our human nature: something that has to do with "role," and something that has to do with the relationships embodied in speech (first, second, and third persons).

Still, if not an essence, might that "something other" be some sort of additional property? Such, of course, is the view of those who say there are some humans who are not persons: to be a person is to have some property beyond mere membership in the human species. But what could that property be? To follow a certain common line of argument, it is the property of awareness of oneself as a subject of experiences.[13] And this line of thought is often developed. But again, the ancient usages suggest the opposite. The person is the actor who takes up a certain role—an activity, not a property. And the person is the human being in the various possible grammatical relationships given by speech.

Sin and Persons, Human and Divine

A notable characteristic of being human is that we speak of our humanity as something capable of being lost. For instance, we describe actions that are particularly vile as "inhumane" and someone who commits them as having "lost" his humanity. What we mean is that, as a person, each of us can live up to, or (conversely) betray, the nature that we have. It's as if our humanity, rather than being a nature that we simply have, is a "role" that we can take up and play well, or lay down. I have spoken earlier about an apple succeeding as an apple: an odd way of talking, to be sure, but pointing to the difference between a good apple and a bad apple. Nonetheless, there is no moral judgment upon an apple that fails to succeed. And therefore we do not speak of apples as persons. By contrast, *there can be moral judgment upon a human being who betrays his humanity.* He may have acted "inhumanly"—for instance, by torturing others. The word "person" speaks to just this point: one may have such a relationship to one's own nature that one is capable of betraying it.

In St. John's Gospel we find the human failure that is sin equated with the refusal to believe in Jesus (see Jn 16.9). This is the discovery of a possibility unknown, it seems, to Platonic thought. For in Plato, the wise man is the one who does what he wills, which he can do because, being wise, what he wants is what is truly good. But this means that he, the wise man, is governed in all he does by reason itself. There is nothing individual about the wise man, for the wise reasoning of anyone is the same as that of anyone else. As Plato sees it, then, if you know the good you will do it. All sin, in this view, stems from ignorance. It would be impossible to know what is good and yet turn your back on it.

But the foundational Christian anthropological insight was just this: that we can know what is good and at the same time reject it. "Wretched man that I am!" cried Saint Paul. That which I want to do, because I know it is good and right, is the very thing I do not do. And what I do not want to do, because I see it is bad and wrong, is nonetheless the thing that I do (see Rom. 7.19-24). Wretched he was, and yet it is a blessed wretchedness. For it is the discovery of the person.

When the gospels speak of the "heart" they are pointing to this special way that human beings relate to their nature. Among many examples, consider these (those with quotation marks are ascribed to Jesus himself):

"For out of the abundance of the heart the mouth speaks" (Mt. 12.34).

"For this people's heart has grown dull" (Mt. 13.15).

"But what comes out of the mouth proceeds from the heart, and this is what defiles" (Mt. 15.18).

"... forgive your brother or sister from your heart" (Mt. 18.35).

He looked around at them with anger; he was grieved at their hardness of heart (Mk 3.5).

But Mary treasured all these words and pondered them in her heart (Lk. 2.19).

"[L]et the one who believes in me drink. As the scripture has said, 'Out of the believer's heart shall flow rivers of living water'" (Jn 7.38).

The gospels, and Jesus in the gospels, speak of the human heart as the ultimate reason for words, actions, and decisions, and the center of the human being. The heart is not the same thing as our human nature, and it does not operate simply on the basis of our human nature. Being the center of the human being (to quote Robert Spaemann), "The heart is its own basis and needs no further basis."[14] The heart reveals that there is something deeper to the human being than human nature, and deeper than any particular quality that any given human being has. The heart, in particular, is deeper than one's rationality, and deeper than one's sense of oneself as a being who has experiences. The heart shows that an individual human being stands to his nature the way an actor stands to his role. Human nature is something we can take up or put down; we can live up to our humanity, or we can turn aside from it. And it is because a human being has a heart, so understood, that a human being is a person.

What then are we saying when we say a human being is a person? We are pointing to something that is true of all human beings: that we are not identical with our nature, and in particular, that there is something to us that is prior to our rationality. We see this when we recognize that humans are able to take up their human nature as a "role" to play—and that, correspondingly, we may fail culpably to live up to our humanity. This possibility is deep within us, is, in fact, the deepest thing about us. It is a discovery made particularly acutely by Christian faith, in that at the very moment that Jesus appears (and thus at the very moment that the offer of salvation appears) the possibility of rejection of Jesus also arises. This capacity to reject, Christians saw, comes from the heart which is something about us that (to repeat) is deeper than our nature and, at the same time, is not a property of ours.

There is now one further step to the argument, and that pertains to the relationality inherent in any "person," which Christians discovered as a deep truth about God himself. It is finally explicit in St. John's Gospel, that Jesus is "the truth" (Jn 14.6). This claim, that truth itself is a person, is not a claim about one person alone. Jesus is the truth because he speaks truthfully everything that he has heard from his Father, and he sends the Spirit of truth who declares everything that Jesus has received from the Father (see, e.g., Jn 8.40, 15.26, 16.13-15). So to speak of the truth is to invoke what Christian theology came to call the Trinity.

We have here, then, two interpersonal realities. One the one hand, there are human interpersonal realities, especially the relationship to Jesus of belief or rejection. These human interpersonal realities show that the decisions of the heart are not decisions about an idea, but about a person who is the ultimate revelation of truth. Truth has appeared on earth as "the unique countenance of another individual person,"[15] a countenance we may adore or even kiss, or from which we may turn away.

But there are also the divine interpersonal realities that constitute God himself. Out of the discovery of the person through the revelation of the heart as the deepest place, where each human being uniquely determines his relationship with truth, which is also, in the Christian claim, his relationship with Jesus, Christians tried to think clearly about these matters, and in doing so they developed an understanding of God according to which he is three "persons" in one "being." God's being or nature is "being" or "nature" only in an analogous sense, for, unlike finite beings, God doesn't *have* his nature, he simply *is* his nature. This stems from the sharp differentiation, a discovery apparently first made by the Jews, that the creator and the creatures cannot have any sort of common measure or be on any sort of continuum.[16] By contrast, consider Plotinus, a non-Christian philosopher influenced by Plato. Plotinus understood the necessary unity of God ("the One"), but unable to think the radical otherness of creator from creature, could only imagine "emanations" from the divine. Thus Plotinus taught that from the One God there emanates Nous (Mind). Then from Nous emanates the World-Soul, and from the World-Soul come creatures. In this neo-platonic world, there are degrees of being, an ontological glissando down from God to our world. The Christian conception was different: it insisted on a sharp line between creator and creatures. The result is that, for Christianity, *the mediations of God all happen within the Godhead himself.* From the Father comes the Word (another name for the Son), and from the Father with the Word comes the Spirit. According to Christian doctrine, both Word and Spirit are God. Spaemann captures it well when he says that each is "the same One another time."[17]

Father, Word, and Spirit are called, in the term taken up in Western Christian thought, Persons. With this usage in place, something remarkable is now at hand to our understanding. For, in the case of the divine Persons, they are three persons with the same "nature." They are different persons with the same essence (as, analogously, we have different human persons with the same human nature). But unlike the differences between human beings, their difference cannot be in any particular property, since the divine Persons have all properties in common. For instance, as the so-called Athanasian Creed has it, the Father is eternal, the Son is eternal, the Spirit is eternal, and "yet they are not three eternals, but one eternal."[18] Any divine attribute applies to each of the Persons.

In short, the intra-trinitarian distinction of Persons is neither by classification nor by property. A Person so understood can be thought of *only* in terms of how he stands with regard to the divine nature, and that is to say, *he can be thought of only in relation to the other Persons.* There could not be a single divine Person. This, analogously, is also the case for created human persons. It is exemplified in the discovery of the ancient grammarians that there is never just one person in speech; if there is a first person, an "I," there is also a second person, a "you," and quite often a third, "him" or "her" or "it." Persons can be thought correctly only in relation to others, that is to say, in plurality.

These understandings were particularly fecund for the development of Christian theology. We could, for instance, go on to contemplate the Incarnation of Christ, whereby one divine Person (the Word) came to have two natures (both human and divine). But we already have enough for our purposes in this Guide. The central point about persons in Christian theology is in fact a revelation that there is more to any individual human than we can ever say. There is a "heart" that escapes description and out of which surprises of action (both creative and destructive) may arise. We can point to human beings; we can name them. We can accept them or reject them. We exist in a fundamental relatedness to them. For there is never an individual person, alone; persons exist always in plurality.

This is the final theological point about persons, that they don't just have relations, they are constituted by their relations.

A Person Is Constituted by Relationships

It is time to spell out the relevance of this argument for the question raised by mentally disabled persons. If to be human means to be an individual creature who has a sense of personal consciousness and agency, then those who have severe mental disabilities cannot be fully human. But if to be human is to be a person, and to be a person is not to be equated with any given property (such as the properties that pertain to human rationality) and, moreover, has to do with plurality (as in the different grammatical persons, none of which can exist without the others), then a way is open for us to understand human beings like "Kelly" to be human and persons just like us. To show this, I will explore how it is that a person is *constituted by* her relationships.

This is radically true for the divine Persons. They have no difference from one another apart from their relationship to one another. As Robert Jenson puts it, "in God ... the persons Father, Son, and Spirit *are* identical with the relations between them; none of the three has any position aloof from his self-giving to or through the others."[19] In recognition of this necessary truth of theology, Aquinas calls each divine person a "subsisting relation."[20]

Yet for human persons this may seem utterly counter-intuitive. I who am writing this book, and you who are reading it, we each understand ourselves as an individual center of consciousness that seeks to understand, to act well, to flourish. Are there ways to help us grasp this claimed feature of being a person, that we are constituted by our relationships?

As a matter of fact, as I have been writing this book, all along I have been imagining you reading it. I have tried, for instance, to anticipate the questions you would have; I have sought to provide examples that would help the text come alive for you. You may well judge that I have done a miserable job in this! Nonetheless, even without knowing you, you have been a sort of presence to me; I have not written this book alone.

Any human communication is the sharing of ideas, concepts, thoughts; we can share them because these ideas are common to us. The more your ideas have been in my mind, the better I will have been able to put my ideas so that they may enter your mind. But even that is a misleading way of putting it, as if our "minds" were individual boxes in and out of which we put ideas. Better, I think, to say that part of what makes me me is the commonality of human thought out of which I have arisen.

Perhaps this will help. Imagine that you lose consciousness for a long period, and when you awaken, you find you have little memory of your past life. Your friends and family, along with your therapists, would be able to help you reconstruct your past to one degree or another (depending on your circumstances). Even if you never recovered your own memories, you could trust your friends to be telling the truth about your past. You would thus find, most explicitly, that who you are is a result of your relationships—that your relationships have given you your identity.

This is not an uncommon experience. Daily, after we sleep, a friend, a spouse, a news reporter, or some other human being will tell us what happened while we were unawake. We receive our being from outside ourselves, even in the trivial sense that we daily appropriate the weather report and build into our lives corresponding anticipations. Sometimes, however, it is far from trivial, as when our spouse informs us that we had a seizure while asleep and need now to go to the doctor for tests.

Here is another instance. A person with an addiction may find himself in the midst of a circle of family and friends. They have all come together to confront him about his addiction. It is an intervention aimed (as is said) "to bring him to himself," to cause him to see the harm that his behavior is doing to himself and others, and to induce him, if possible, to accept freely a course of action that may save him. That circle of friends and family is attempting to bring self-awareness to an individual who lacks it.

Less dramatically, a friend may tell you that you have acted badly toward someone, although you had no conscious intention to do so. You were unaware of the real effects of your behavior; your friend has helped you to see better who you are.

And conversely, a friend may point out to you your moral virtues, that they are better developed than you thought. She may identify particular habits of friendship that you have cultivated, positive steps that now, since she has pointed them out, are reinforced and you are more likely to build upon them.

In general, our unconsciousness of our selves, whether (as in the above examples) from injury, or sleep, or addiction, or inattention, or inexperience, or from something not yet mentioned—our unconsciousness points to the reality that who we are is not identical with who we think we are. Here, I believe, is a strong clue that the theological claim is true, that we human persons are constituted by our relationships. For all those things about me of which I am unconscious, they are embedded in relationships with others and they can be revealed to me by others (although the process will never be complete).

A Final Word about "Kelly"

So it can make sense to recognize as persons, that is, as human beings just like us, folks like "Kelly" who, as far as we can tell, will never have a sense of self as an agent acting in the world. For what matters is the relationships of human beings with one another. Kelly is Kelly because the folks who live with her have friendship with her. Reinders would say that we are human beings because someone else has befriended us. Our relationships constitute us as persons.

This is not to deny the Christian hope that, in the resurrection at the last day, each of us will receive a "body," which will be manifestly our own body and yet something "glorious." So, as far as we are able to understand, we would expect the glorified body to be unimpaired either physically or mentally. We would expect, then, that Kelly's resurrected body would have what is necessary for her to have a sense of a self who lives in the giving and receiving of friendship.

But this does not render her happiness as entirely postmortem. For in the meantime, in the concreteness of this present life, Kelly has been befriended, and as such she is already a real human being, a person constituted by her relationships. That she is unable to be conscious of herself as a recipient of friendship does not make these relationships unreal.

And a Final Word about All of Us

The theological understanding of "person" grounds the claim of Christian ethics that our humanity is both task and gift. The goal of ethics, I have claimed, is to succeed as a human being—to be happy—to engage in activities that embody and advance human excellence. These moral virtues bring our affections in line with our reason and our will in line with the common good. And they are capped by the virtue of good sense—and, also, transformed by gifts of grace, supremely the gift of charity. So the highest goal of Christian ethics—and the highest fulfillment of the human being, happiness in its true sense—is in the excellence of charity, friendship with God and with others.

Jesus—may I say it one last time?—is the first human being so to live entirely by love, in friendship with God and with all and every human being. No one reading this Guide, and certainly not its author, has achieved such full and true happiness. We are at best only on the way, our excellences still under development. We might rightly say that we are only partially successful at being human. But our humanity, while it requires our free choice to undertake the virtues, is not primarily our task—and it is flat impossible for it to be our *individual* task. Our humanity is a gift—a gift received from our friends, a gift we too may sometimes bestow upon our friends; the gift in the end of friendship with God. It is so because we are persons.

* * *

Notes for Further Reading

Stanley Hauerwas has a number of essays on disability which, like all his work, provide unexpected insight as well as intellectual delight. See, for instance, "Must a Patient Be a Person to Be a Patient? Or, My Uncle Charlie Is Not Much of a Person But He Is Still My Uncle Charlie," in Stanley Hauerwas, *Truthfulness and Tragedy* (Notre Dame, Ind.: University of Notre Dame Press, 1977), 127–31. With regard to disability, Hauerwas's project is to show that if we look squarely at what is implied by the existence of people with disabilities we will see the presumptions of modernity radically undermined. In particular, we will see that none of us starts out as an autonomous individual who enters into engagement with other free and autonomous individuals as we choose. But rather, we humans are dependent creatures, related to one another and reliant upon the author of our lives, from the beginning and throughout, without end. See, for instance, the essays in Part III of *Truthfulness and Tragedy*.

On a thoughtfully personal level, the meaning of living with the disabled is explored in a late work of Henri Nouwen's, the Catholic priest and noted author of many books in spirituality. See his *Adam: God's Beloved* (Maryknoll, N.Y.: Orbis Books, 1997). Nouwen, weary of the academic life, had moved to live in the l'Arche community in Toronto. The challenges of taking care of Adam transformed into gifts that he, Nouwen, received in what turned out to be the closing years of his life: *Adam*, published posthumously, is Nouwen's final book.

The reader who wishes to study particular moral "bioethical" issues such as abortion, euthanasia, eugenics, and the like might well turn to Agneta Sutton, *Bioethics: A Guide for the Perplexed* (London: T & T Clark, 2008).

The middle section of Reinders's book develops a robust theological anthropology based on the understanding of a person that has been sketched in this chapter. There the reader will find exposition and analysis of the pertinent thinking of Karl Barth and John D. Zizioulas on persons as relations. See Hans S. Reinders, *Receiving the Gift of Friendship: Profound Disability, Theological Anthropology, and Ethics* (Grand Rapids, Mich.: Eerdmans, 2008). Robert W. Jenson also has argued that we cannot understand being human apart from taking the Trinity seriously. See his *On Thinking the Human: Resolutions of Difficult Notions* (Grand Rapids, Mich.: Eerdmans, 2003).

NOTES

Chapter One

1　Charles L. Stevenson, "The Emotive Meaning of Ethical Terms," in David E. Cooper ed. *Ethics: The Classic Readings* (Oxford: Blackwell Publishers, 1998), 264–80; here, 279.

2　Alban McCoy makes this argument in his book, *An Intelligent Person's Guide to Christian Ethics* (London: Continuum, 2004), 28–9.

3　And also no guilt. Already academic psychologists, under the influence of neuroscience, can be found arguing that no one should be held legally responsible for actions caused by abnormal brain structures. (I am grateful to James Cornwell for this observation.)

4　See Herbert McCabe, *God Matters* (Geoffrey Chapman, 1987; repr. London: Continuum, 2005), 12.

5　Faced with a victim, students typically do modify their initial embrace of subjectivism. Ethics is subjective, they will say, in all matters in which no one is hurt. One might think that no one is really hurt when office paper is taken by an employee—or when music is illegally downloaded from the internet. And thus, in such cases, whether the action in question is right or wrong is a matter of one's subjective ethics. Nonetheless, even were such cases to be set aside, if in other matters there still remained victims—then subjectivism would have failed to undermine ethics. For when there are victims, we can use our reason to discern what the harm is and to identify it as truly, and not merely subjectively, a harm.

6　Although they do not affect the argument here, there are problematics with the concept of conscience. I take them up in Chapter 5.

7　For this, David Noel Freedman ed. *Eerdmans Dictionary of the Bible* (Grand Rapids, Mich.: Eerdmans, 2000), s.v. "Logos."

8　See Augustine, *Confessions*, Book V.

9   For a contemporary account, see McCabe, *God Matters*, ch. 1,
    "Creation." For a classic account, see Aquinas, *Summa theologiae*
    I.2.3. (For more on the *Summa*, including an explanation of this
    notation, see the Notes for Further Reading at the end of Chapter
    4.) Aquinas's passage on God's existence is reprinted widely, for
    instance in Aquinas, *Selected Philosophical Writings* (selected and
    trans. Timothy McDermott; Oxford: Oxford University Press, 1993),
    199–202.

10 Joseph Ratzinger, *Church, Ecumenism, and Politics* (New York:
    Crossroad, 1988), 153.

11 Benedict XVI, "Faith, Reason, and the University: Memories and
    Reflections," http://www.vatican.va/holy_father/benedict_xvi/
    speeches/2006/september/documents/hf_ben-xvi_spe_20060912_
    university-regensburg_en.html (accessed March 23, 2011).

12 Although it will take generations before the pontificate of John
    Paul II can be properly evaluated, we can already appreciate this
    development. Instead of defending the rights of the church against
    error, John Paul defended the intrinsic rights of all human beings.
    These universal human rights, in turn, he understood to have
    been given by the Incarnation, in which the Son of God became a
    human being. See George Weigel, *The End and the Beginning* (New
    York: Doubleday, 2010). See also Victor Lee Austin, "John Paul
    II's Ironic Legacy in Political Theology," *Pro Ecclesia* 16 (2007):
    165–94.

Chapter Two

1   See Lev. 19.18, and Mk 12.29-31 and parallels. For the parable of
    the good Samaritan, see Lk. 10.29-37.

2   As does the prodigal son; see Lk. 15.17 for the phrase.

3   Stanley Hauerwas, *A Community of Character* (Notre Dame, Ind.:
    University of Notre Dame Press, 1981), 10.

4   See Herbert McCabe, *The Good Life: Ethics and the Pursuit of
    Happiness* (ed. Brian Davies; London: Continuum, 2005), 73–8.

5   McCabe, *God Matters*, 19.

6   The classic declaration was made by the fourth ecumenical council,
    in Chalcedon in A.D. 451: the two natures (divine and human) are
    "without confusion, without change, without division, without
    separation."

7 "It is not possible that God and the universe should add up to make two... . If God is the cause of everything, there is nothing that he is alongside." McCabe, *God Matters*, 6.

8 "The truth is that only in the mystery of the incarnate Word [Jesus Christ] does the mystery of man take on light. For Adam, the first man, was a figure of him who was to come, namely, Christ the Lord. Christ, the final Adam, by the revelation of the mystery of the Father and His love, fully reveals man to man himself and makes his supreme calling clear." *Gaudium et spes* 22; in Walter M. Abbott ed. *The Documents of Vatican II* (New York: Guild Press, 1966), 220.

9 The following paragraphs summarize a much more detailed argument made by Herbert McCabe in *Law, Love, and Language* (Sheed and Ward, 1968; repr. London: Continuum, 2003), ch. 1–3. Also see McCabe, *The Good Life*, ch. 3–4.

10 Thus it was inevitable: Jesus had to die. See McCabe, "Good Friday: The Mystery of the Cross," in *God Matters*, 90–100. "As I see it, not Adam but Jesus was the first human being, the first member of the human race in whom humanity came to fulfillment, the first human being for whom to live was simply to love—for this is what human beings are for. The aim of human life is to live in friendship—a friendship amongst ourselves which in fact depends on a friendship, or covenant, that God has established between ourselves and him." Ibid., 93.

Chapter Three

1 As in Alasdair MacIntyre, *After Virtue* (Notre Dame, Ind.: University of Notre Dame Press, 2nd edn, 1984). See, e.g., the opening of his second chapter: "The most striking feature of contemporary moral utterance is that so much of it is used to express disagreements; and the most striking feature of the debates in which these disagreements are expressed is their interminable character." Ibid., 6. MacIntyre's title indicates both his analysis of the contemporary situation and his diagnosis. We exist in a world that has forgotten and is ignorant of (is "after" in the sense of "post") an old tradition of virtue, and it is virtue that we need to recover (to go "after" in the sense of to "seek"). Much ethical thought in the ensuing decades has gone after virtue.

2 Immanuel Kant, *The Fundamental Principles of the Metaphysic of Ethics* (trans. Otto Manthey-Zorn; New York: Appleton-Century,

1938), 8. This work, *Grundlegung zur Metaphysik der Sitten*, is translated under a number of titles involving the various permutations of "Fundamental Principles" or "Foundations" or "Groundwork"; "Metaphysic" or "Metaphysics"; and "Ethics" or "Morals."

3   Kant, *Fundamental Principles*, 17; emphasis in original.

4   To draw out the logic more explicitly: I would be trying to say both (1) I may steal whenever I can get away with it, and (2) all other people may steal when they can get away with it. But the reason for (1) will have something to do with my desire to possess and take use of that which I steal. Stealing only makes sense when there is an institution of private property in the background. But (2) implies that others could take it away from me when I'm not looking. Therefore (2) undermines the purpose of (1). Therefore (1) turns out not to be universalizable.

5   *The Bhagavad Gita* (trans. W. J. Johnson; Oxford: Oxford University Press, 1994), ch. 1, vv. 26–7; in Cooper ed. *Ethics: The Classic Readings*, 93–109. Subsequent citations to chapter and verse are given in the text.

6   Jon D. Levenson, *The Death and Resurrection of the Beloved Son: The Transformation of Child Sacrifice in Judaism and Christianity* (New Haven: Yale University Press, 1993), 125–42.

7   John Stuart Mill, *Utilitarianism* (ed. George Sher; Indianapolis, Ind.: Hackett, 2nd edn, 2001), 7.

8   Mill, *Utilitarianism*, 8.

9   Ibid., 9, 10. For more on epistemic authority, see Victor Lee Austin, *Up with Authority: Why We Need Authority to Flourish as Human Beings* (London: T & T Clark, 2010), ch. 3.

10 Speaking of the Roman Catholic ethical school of "proportionalism," Jean Porter writes: "[T]he success of this program for moral analysis requires a convincing standard of commensuration by which we can determine which of a number of possible concrete outcomes really does count as the lesser evil or the greater good. The proportionalists are (wisely) reluctant to adopt the utilitarian strategy of analyzing all benefits and harms in terms of a single standard of well-being, but they have not come up with a convincing alternative, or even one single alternative that is acceptable to most proportionalists themselves." Jean Porter, *The Recovery of Virtue: The Relevance of Aquinas for Christian Ethics* (Louisville, Ky.: Westminster/John Knox Press, 1990), 20.

11 Mill, *Utilitarianism*, 11; emphasis in original.

12 Mill, *Utilitarianism*, 11.

13 Mill, *Utilitarianism*, 17.

14 Kant, *Fundamental Principles*, 15.

15 Joseph Fletcher, *Situation Ethics: The New Morality* (Philadelphia: Westminster Press, 1965). I quote from the back cover of the 15th printing, 1975; emphasis in original.

16 Fletcher, unlike Mill, evidences optimism about the possibility of calculating which course of action is the most loving (which is, equivalently, to provide the most justice or the greatest good), thus rejecting any claim that differing goods could be incommensurable. "It is possible that by learning how to assign numerical values to the factors at stake in problems of conscience, love's calculations can gain accuracy in an ethical *ars major*." Fletcher, *Situation Ethics*, 118.

17 The name commonly given to Mt. 22.37-40, recited as part of the communion rite of the Book of Common Prayer of Fletcher's Protestant Episcopal Church. See also Jesus' claim not to overthrow the law but to fulfill it, Mt. 5.17.

18 Fletcher, *Situation Ethics*, 91.

19 Nigel Biggar, for instance, judges that in certain (fortunately rare) situations of intractable pain it is morally permissible deliberately to kill another human being. Notwithstanding this conclusion, however, he also holds that such actions should not be legalized or generally countenanced, because of the negative social effects that we have good reason to anticipate would ensue. Nigel Biggar, *Aiming to Kill* (Cleveland, Ohio: Pilgrim Press, 2004).

20 Aristotle, *The Nicomachean Ethics* (trans. H. Rackham; Loeb Classical Library; Cambridge, Mass.: Harvard University Press, rev. edn, 1934), I.i (1094a1-2).

21 This summary formulation is from Hippocrates G. Apostle trans. *Aristotle's Nichomachean Ethics* (Grinnell, Iowa: Peripatetic Press, 1984), p. xiii; summarizing I.vii (1098a16-19).

22 In various forms, this thought-experiment is proposed by Robert Spaemann, John Finnis, and others; Herbert McCabe attributes it to Robert Nozick. See, e.g., Robert Spaemann, *Basic Moral Concepts* (trans. T. J. Armstrong; London: Routledge, 1989), 19.

Chapter Four

1   The following discussion is influenced by an argument advanced by Herbert McCabe in various places. See, e.g., McCabe, *God Matters*, ch. 3, "Evil."

2   See Thomas Aquinas, *Summa theologiae*, I-II.1.2. And see Porter, *The Recovery of Virtue*, 69–72.

3   After Jesus, by Christian doctrine, the possibility of being fully human is open to all human beings. It may have been achieved by his mother, Mary; that claim is tied up with the particularly Roman Catholic dogmas of her Immaculate Conception and Assumption. But her conception can only have been immaculate (and thus her humanity undiminished by sin) by virtue of an out-of-time (proleptic) gift to her of the benefits of the salvation wrought in Jesus. Such an eschatologically-grounded understanding has promise of being ecumenically acceptable. See "Mary: Grace and Hope in Christ. The Seattle Statement of the Anglican-Roman Catholic International Commission" (text with commentaries and study guide; ed. Donald Bolen and Gregory Cameron; London: Continuum, 2006), particularly sections 58–63.

4   *Gaudium et spes* 22; in Abbott ed. *The Documents of Vatican II*, 220.

5   See Thomas Aquinas, *Summa theologiae* I-II.94.2; discussed in Porter, *Recovery of Virtue*, 89. Herbert McCabe connects the inclinations with deep desires that are common to all people: "the deep desires that a man has, the desires he cannot help having, are a manifestation of his human life. His being human consists in his having what Aquinas calls these 'natural inclinations.'" McCabe, *Law, Love, and Language*, 63.

6   I follow Porter in making the fundamental human inclinations four in number; in the cited Aquinas passage, the last two (living in society and knowing the truth about God) are linked as one. They are, however, distinguishable in thought, and to separate them out allows me to make two points. First, that humans are in fact inclined by their nature to knowledge of truth, and that this is, speaking simply in terms of created nature, the highest thing about humans. Second, to know the truth *about God* is a reminder that Christian ethics understands creation to have been reestablished in Christ. To know God as Christ knows God is *now* the end of the human creature. This latter point is significant for the discussion of infused cardinal virtues, which I take up in the following chapter.

7   According to R. E. Houser, the specification of these four as the four fundamental virtues comes from Plato. But it was Ambrose, the fourth-century bishop of Milan, who first labeled them "cardinal." See Houser's article on the virtue of courage in Stephen J. Pope ed. *The Ethics of Aquinas* (Washington, D.C.: Georgetown University Press, 2002), 304–20 (304–6).

8   In Books III–V of the *Nicomachean Ethics*, Aristotle takes up, in this order: courage, temperance, liberality, magnificence, pride, ambition, good temper, friendliness, truthfulness, ready wit, and justice. These are the moral virtues. In Book VI we find the intellectual virtues: science, art, practical wisdom, intuitive reason, and philosophic wisdom.

9   See Porter, *Recovery of Virtue*, 121.

10 The usage can be seen in Aristotle, *Nicomachean Ethics*, II.1. Aristotle, as noted above, has quite a number of moral virtues in addition to these three.

11 Porter, *Recovery of Virtue*, 111.

12 For the classical discussion, see *Nicomachean Ethics* VII.1-10. In Aquinas, see *Summa theologiae* II-II.155-6. Porter develops this matter in *Recovery of Virtue*, 114–15.

13 Aristotle has it that both the unjust person and the unjust act are unequal; that is, to be unfair is simply to be unequal. Aristotle distinguishes two types of justice (which he calls "commutative" and "rectificatory") as the distinction between two forms of equality: geometrical and arithmetical. Whether this is enlightening is debated; alas, the fact of the debate suggests that it isn't. See *Nicomachean Ethics* V.3-4.

14 Yet one might wonder if the notion of fundamental human equality is sustainable without theological ground. Following, e.g., the thought of Nigel Biggar, we could see this as a place where Christians and others have overlapping common ground, but the Christian also has, in addition, substantive content given by Christian faith. For the Christian will hold that all alike have sinned, that all alike are offered redemption, and that every human being is a potential friend of God. Such theological convictions can broaden one's view of who counts as a fellow human being, while they also can help motivate sustained action in which the excellence of justice comes to play. See Biggar, *Behaving in Public*, ch. 2.

15 This is Porter's formulation of Aquinas's view, in Porter, *Recovery of Virtue*, 124. The following account is largely indebted to her treatment.

16 So Porter, *Recovery of Virtue*, 124. See Aquinas, *Summa theologiae* II-II.58.5-6.

17 So Porter summarizes it, at *Recovery of Virtue*, 129.

18 Herbert McCabe, *Law, Love, and Language*, 7–8.

19 For detail, see Porter, *Recovery of Virtue*, 131.

20 *Summa theologiae* II-II.66.8. Aquinas distinguishes robbery from theft, holding the former to be worse as it is done openly, while theft is secret. Although an interesting distinction for his purposes, in this Guide the words are used interchangeably.

21 See *Summa theologiae* II-II.66.7.

22 Josef Pieper, *The Four Cardinal Virtues* (Notre Dame, Ind.: University of Notre Dame Press, 1966), 73–75, 113.

23 Distributive justice appears in but two of the 65 Questions that Aquinas devoted to the virtue in the *Summa theologiae*, namely, II-II.61.1-3 and II-II.63. For further discussion, see Porter, *Recovery of Virtue*, 152–4.

24 For this and the following discussion, see Oliver O'Donovan, *The Ways of Judgment* (Grand Rapids, Mich.: Eerdmans, 2005), 33–40.

25 See O'Donovan, *Ways of Judgment*, 38.

Chapter Five

1 Herbert McCabe, "Aquinas on Good Sense," in *God Still Matters* (ed. Brian Davies; London: Continuum, 2003), 152–65 (152).

2 William C. Mattison III, *Introducing Moral Theology: True Happiness and the Virtues* (Grand Rapids, Mich.: Brazos Press, 2008), 97.

3 McCabe, *God Still Matters*, 153.

4 The use of the terms "truth-preserving" and "satisfactoriness-preserving" as corresponding to theoretical and practical reasoning, respectively, is drawn from Anthony Kenny. See McCabe, *God Still Matters*, 160.

5 "This is a very peculiar word... . It is, for one thing, a piece of fake Greek that seems to have been invented by Latin-speaking medieval philosophers and does not occur in any classical Greek text." McCabe, *God Still Matters*, 158. Timothy E. O'Connell says the invention of the word was likely Jerome's doing, working from an imperfectly legible Greek manuscript of the Bible. See O'Connell, *Principles for a Catholic Morality* (San Francisco: Harper and Row, rev. edn, 1990), 109–10.

6   McCabe, *God Still Matters*, 159.

7   McCabe, *God Still Matters*, 160.

8   How could he make this error? Perhaps he's on drugs. Or perhaps his name is Jacob (see Gen. 29.18-25).

9   See Aquinas, *Summa theologiae*, I-II.19.5-6.

10   McCabe, *God Still Matters*, 156.

11   What action is then available? "One can withdraw from the error," as Oliver O'Donovan quotes Aquinas. "The very possibility of moral thinking transforms our experience of the conscience, which is directed to forming judgments, not delivering commands." Oliver O'Donovan, *Church in Crisis* (Eugene, Ore.: Cascade Books, 2008), 31–2. Of course, to know the error as such and to be able to withdraw from it may require such perspectival content and motivation as are given by the theological and infused virtues, particularly charity—as this chapter goes on to discuss.

12   Aquinas says that such a person has cunning rather than good sense. For him, the virtues necessarily aim at the true human good, and anything that looks like a virtue but aims at something bad or evil is a false virtue. For this point made regarding good sense, see *Summa theologiae* I-II.57.5.

13   In the prototypical story of Genesis 3–4, as soon as the first humans rebel against God, the man blames the woman, the soil turns hard, and within a generation fratricide occurs. Thus we have alienation from God, from one another, and from the environment. Furthermore, their "knowledge" of their nakedness and the need for clothing is symbolic of self-alienation.

14   In this regard, see, in the notes for further reading at the end of Chapter 2, the comments on specifically Christian contributions to ethics in Nigel Biggar, *Behaving in Public*.

15   In one of his cheerier moments, Augustine famously said that kingdoms in this world of sin are no better than legalized piracy. See Augustine, *City of God* IV.4.

16   See Aquinas, *Summa theologiae* I-II.62.1.

17   For this argument generally, see Herbert McCabe, *God Matters*, ch. 1, "Creation"; and Herbert McCabe, *God Still Matters*, ch. 2, "The Logic of Mysticism."

18   For the following discussion I am largely indebted to Brian Davies, *The Thought of Thomas Aquinas* (Oxford: Clarendon Press, 1992), ch. 14, "The Heart of Grace."

19 See Davies, *The Thought of Thomas Aquinas*, 279–80. Some say, however, that there is a fiduciary element in all knowledge, which would make the difference between faith in God and the botanist's knowledge of plants a matter of degree, not of kind. See, for an excellent example, Michael Polanyi, *Personal Knowledge: Towards a Post-Critical Philosophy* (Chicago: University of Chicago Press, corr. edn, 1962).

20 The Latin version of the Nicene Creed makes a distinction between believing in and simply believing. In speaking this creed, one states one's belief "in" God the Father Almighty, and "in" Jesus Christ his only Son, and "in" the Holy Spirit, but a bit later one says simply "I believe one holy catholic and apostolic Church." This distinction was preserved in the traditional English of the Book of Common Prayer.

21 An instance of this was sketched above in Chapter 2. If it is said that it is a contradiction for Jesus to have two natures, theology can reply as follows. It would be a contradiction for any human being to have, in addition to his human nature, some other created nature. So it would be a contradiction to be both a man and a duck. No one can be 100% human and 100% duck. But the divine nature is not a created nature. So the claim that Jesus has human and divine natures, that he is 100% human and 100% divine, is not the self-contradiction of a being having two created natures. Of course, since the divine nature is no created nature, we can have no positive understanding of what it means! The best we can do is to discern the failure of the argument that being both divine and human is self-contradictory.

22 This example is given by Davies, *The Thought of Thomas Aquinas*, 284.

23 Aquinas, *Summa theologiae* I-II.62.3.

24 See (again) Mt. 22.37-40; Mk 12.29-33; Lk. 10.25-28. The Johannine version is to equate love of Jesus and love of one another, which results in the Father loving the disciple and the Father and Jesus dwelling in the disciple. See, e.g., Jn 15.12 and 14.23.

25 Bonnie Kent, "Habits and Virtues," in Stephen J. Pope ed. *The Ethics of Aquinas*, 116–30 (122).

26 This is Aquinas's own example; see *Summa theologiae* I-II.63.4.

27 A comprehensive treatment of this matter is given by Stephen Loughlin, "Thomas Aquinas and the Importance of Fasting to the Christian Life," *Pro Ecclesia* 17 (2008): 343–61.

28 See *Gaudium et spes* 22.

29 *Summa theologiae* I-II.92.1 reply to obj. 1. Here I quote from the translation by Richard J. Regan in Aquinas, *On Law, Morality, and Politics* (Indianapolis, Ind.: Hackett Publishing, 2nd edn, 2002).

30 Kent, "Habits and Virtues," 126; footnote in the original omitted. Kent cites Aquinas, *Summa theologiae* I-II.65.3.

31 Here is the broad theological question of the relationship of grace and works. If I may make a brief comment, it seems to me that this discussion often is carried on without regard for the radical difference of divine action from human action. Since God causes everything that exists to exist for as long as it exists and exactly in the way that it does exist, God causes my free actions. Yet this causation does not take away my freedom: God causes my free actions precisely to be free. Like most things when we talk about God, this conclusion cannot be comprehended, although we can see the necessity of affirming it. It thus strikes me, with regard to the so-called dialectic of grace and free will, that it would be helpful if we remembered that God's giving something to us does not *per se* remove our freedom. The causalities involved—human and divine— are non-competitive.

32 At least in Bonnie Kent's reading, which she puts forward as a progressive development within Aquinas's thought. See Kent, "Habits and Virtues," 123.

33 See Mt. 25:31-46.

34 For instance, St. Benedict (c. 480–c. 547), whose Rule has shaped Western monasticism to this day, "made care of the sick a paramount duty of his monks." David Bentley Hart, *Atheist Delusions: The Christian Revolution and Its Fashionable Enemies* (New Haven: Yale University Press, 2009), 30.

Chapter Six

1 As the *Ethics* comes to us, friendship is the topic of Books VIII and IX, following the virtues as discussed in Books II–VII.

2 At Matt. 20.13, 22.12, and 26.50, the Greek word here translated "friend" is a form of *hetairos*, whereas in all the other New Testament cases that I cite the Greek is a form of *philos* instead. Since both words spread themselves over a range of meaning—as does the English word "friend" itself—it is not clear that a case can be made for a firm distinction between them. But *hetairos* is unique to Matthew and is used solely to remonstrate—thus, a difference of

context, not of meaning. See Robert H. Gundry, *Matthew* (Grand Rapids, Mich.: Eerdmans, 2nd edn, 1994), 398.

3   Thus the Revised Standard Version. In the New Revised Standard Version, by contrast, it is taken as an imperative: "Friend, do what you are here to do." Translations have gone back and forth over whether this is a command or a question; the nineteenth-century Textus Receptus makes it a question. If it were taken as a command, still the parallel with the previously noted parables would remain, but without the interrogative commonality.

4   For a valuable and meticulously detailed study that deserves wider notice, see E. D. H. (Liz) Carmichael, *Friendship: Interpreting Christian Love* (London: T & T Clark, 2004).

5   See Augustine, *City of God* XIV.28.

6   Lienhard identifies Augustine's new definition of friendship as given at *Confessions* IV.iv.7: "There is no true friendship unless you establish it as a bond between souls that cleave to each other through the love 'poured out into our hearts by the Holy Spirit who is given to us'." See Joseph Lienhard, "Friendship, Friends," in *Augustine through the Ages: An Encyclopedia* (ed. Allan D. Fitzgerald; Grand Rapids, Mich.: Eerdmans, 2009), 372–3.

7   In those days, children of Christian parents were often not baptized until later in life. They would be enrolled as catechumens, i.e., candidates for baptism, but the baptism ceremony itself was postponed, on account of a strong understanding that baptism washed away all sins and thus, after baptism, sins were a terrible thing, difficult to deal with. Baptism near death would remove a lifetime's worth of sins.

8   *Confessions* IV.iv.9. I am quoting from Henry Chadwick's translation: Saint Augustine, *Confessions* (Oxford: Oxford University Press, 1991).

9   Augustine was a great rhetorician and, as a bishop, often involved in controversies. His *Confessions* is doubtless shaped by a desire to show himself an orthodox Christian, while at the same time the *Confessions* itself is shaping what orthodox Christianity is. It is not necessary to hold that Augustine gives a full and accurate account of his friendship in order to see what he wants to teach about friendship.

10   See Augustine, *Confessions* IV.ix.14. He would, of course, need to understand the friendship, if it were a true one, as having been given by God, as a grace of the Holy Spirit.

11   Carmichael, *Friendship*, 66–7.

12 As he does, e.g., at *Summa theologiae* II-II.23.1. Other theologians
    had "identified" charity and friendship, as early as John Cassian
    of the 4th/5th centuries; before him, some Greek theologians had
    "associated" the two. So Daniel Schwartz, *Aquinas on Friendship*
    (Oxford: Clarendon Press, 2007), 5.

13 Carmichael, *Friendship*, 101, 105. She explains that Aquinas's
    uniqueness stems from the availability of a complete Latin edition
    of the *Nicomachean Ethics*, which had come out for the first time
    when he was in his early 20s. Aristotle's work made it both possible
    and necessary for Aquinas to equate charity and friendship. See also
    Schwartz, *Aquinas on Friendship*, 5. One may note, in this regard,
    the use of Aristotle's analysis of true friendship as involving love,
    well-wishing (or benevolence, desiring the good), and mutuality
    founded in communication or communion of some kind. See again
    Summa theologiae II-II.23.1.

14 For more detail on the following arguments, see Carmichael,
    Friendship, 105–26.

15 Aquinas makes this point in connection with love of enemies: we
    love our enemies because they, too, belong to God (in that God's
    love extends to his enemies). *Summa theologiae* II-II.23.1, reply to
    obj. 2. See also *Summa theologiae* II-II.25.1. Here and following,
    unattributed translations of the *Summa theologiae* are taken from
    Saint Thomas Aquinas, *The Summa Theologica* (2 vols, trans.
    Fathers of the English Dominican Province, rev. Daniel J. Sullivan;
    Great Books of the Western World; Chicago: Encyclopaedia
    Britannica, 1950).

16 Aquinas, *Summa theologiae* I-II.65.5.

17 Aquinas, *Summa theologiae* II-II.25.8.

18 In *Summa theologiae* II-II.25.12, Aquinas concludes that there
    are three right objects of love in friendship: God, our neighbor,
    and ourselves. God is the source of all happiness, and thus loved;
    both our neighbor and ourselves can be loved as being, at least
    potentially, partakers of that happiness. In addition, although not
    a proper object of our love, our bodies can receive happiness "by a
    kind of overflow." So we have a proper respect for our bodies, but it
    is less than friendship (love in charity); it is nonetheless love. *Summa
    theologiae* II-II.25.5.

19 Aquinas, *Summa theologiae* II-II.25.8.

20 Schwartz, however, concludes that although Aquinas's notion of
    friendship can include disagreement and wide diversity, nonetheless
    "Aquinas never dilutes or relaxes other ... requirements of

friendship such as good-willing mutual love. This good-willing love which includes mutual concern, and the disposition to help others, is central to any notion of friendship." Schwartz, *Aquinas on Friendship*, 164.

21 I use "heaven" here as the customary shorthand for the environment of persons in the post-resurrection state who enjoy the Lord. It is, however, a potentially misleading term. See N. T. Wright, *Surprised by Hope: Rethinking Heaven, Resurrection, and the Mission of the Church* (New York: HarperOne, 2008).

22 Aquinas, *Selected Philosophical Writings*, 192.

23 For this point, N. T. Wright, *Surprised by Hope*, 43–4.

Chapter Seven

1 Terminology, here, can be a touchy business. I will use the term "disabled" as a generic, middle-of-the-road designation, without the specificity of terms that once were common but are now sensed as cruel ("retarded" or "crippled," for instance), but recognizing its own awkwardness (the way the term has been construed to mean that a person with a disability is thereby less of a person). The reader should bear in mind that the argument being made in this chapter affirms the full humanity of disabled people. Which is to say, we do not need delicately to avoid facing the full reality of any sort of disability; our humanity is not so weak that it won't survive the examination.

2 The Scriptures refer to such cases as demonic possession. One can be agnostic about the existence of demons and still recognize the liberating force of Jesus' healing.

3 Some people have found it surprising to learn that it is, in fact, official Roman Catholic doctrine (and not merely the speculation of certain theologians) that every human being is offered, during his or her life, access to the salvation wrought in Christ. The identification of the means by which this offer is extended is an open question, and an important project for creative theological exploration. Regarding the offer of salvation in Christ as universally made, see the Vatican II Pastoral Constitution *Gaudium et spes* 22: "since Christ died for all men, and since the ultimate vocation of man is in fact one, and divine, we ought to believe that the Holy Spirit in a manner known only to God offers to every man the possibility of being associated with this paschal mystery." Abbott ed. *The*

Documents of Vatican II, 221–2 (the "only" is not in the Latin). For an argument concerning development of the contemporary issue as a theological task, see Thomas Joseph White, "On the Universal Possibility of Salvation," *Pro Ecclesia* 17 (2008): 269–80.

4 See the astute observations and reflections of the neurologist Oliver Sacks in his *Seeing Voices: A Journey into the World of the Deaf* (Berkeley, Calif.: University of California Press, 1989; repr. New York: Vintage, 2000). Sacks speaks of "the unique spatial syntax and grammar" of Sign, of "its unique linguistic use of space," of the powers of "language in four dimensions," of its essentially "cinematic" character; see pp. 69–71 and, more generally, the chapter "Thinking in Sign." At Mount Aloysius College, my theology students who were majoring in Interpreter Training (i.e., sign language interpreters) would vigorously debate the propriety of the cochlear implant. If you could be cured of your deafness—if indeed the cure were complete and unproblematic (as, currently, it is not)—*should you avail yourself of it?* Although my students would grant that deafness was a disability, they would not agree that it should be cured. They could sense that something human would thereby be lost.

5 Hans S. Reinders, *Receiving the Gift of Friendship: Profound Disability, Theological Anthropology, and Ethics* (Grand Rapids, Mich.: Eerdmans, 2008), 20–1.

6 Michael Tooley, "Abortion and Infanticide," *Philosophy and Public Affairs* 2 (1972): 37–65. Peter Singer has derived both fame and notoriety from making this argument.

7 The practice of the exposure of children is also in the background of Chinua Achebe's widely-read book, *Things Fall Apart* (New York: Anchor Books, 1994). This tragic novel derives haunting power, in part, from its sympathetic capturing of the attractiveness of Christianity to those who mourned the loss of their exposed children, while also showing that Christianity's arrival precipitates the downfall of the preexisting culture; because of its coming, things will fall apart.

8 Although not a work in ethics, Jean-Dominique Bauby's memoir, *The Diving-Bell and the Butterfly* (trans. Jeremy Leggatt; New York: Alfred A. Knopf, 1997), is a strong testament to the undiminished humanity of a man with "locked-in syndrome." Bauby, who had been a fashion magazine editor, now could do nothing but blink one of his eyelids. With the patient help of his therapist, who worked out a way for him to "write" by "blinking" when she uttered the letter he wanted, Bauby wrote the following of an encounter in a

fashionable Parisian restaurant that some friends had overheard (p. 82): "The gossipers were as greedy as vultures who have just discovered a disemboweled antelope. 'Did you know that Bauby is now a total vegetable?' said one. 'Yes, I heard. A complete vegetable,' came the reply. The word 'vegetable' must have tasted sweet on the know-it-all's tongue, for it came up several times between mouthfuls of Welsh rarebit. The tone of voice left no doubt that henceforth I belonged on a vegetable stall and not to the human race." Although the diners' use of the word "vegetable" was, in this case, incorrect, it reveals the point of the usage.

9   The Catholic moral theologian Charles Camosy has made it a point to take Peter Singer's arguments seriously and to build bridges of dialogue with him. This is good work, and there needs to be more of it. Dialogue, of course, does not mean compromise of principles, but rather a probing of depths. Camosy and Singer jointly organized, with others, the "Open Hearts, Open Minds" conference on abortion, held at Princeton in 2010.

10 For the remainder of this section and the one to follow, I have been deeply instructed by Robert Spaemann, *Persons: The Difference between "Someone" and "Something"* (trans. Oliver O'Donovan; Oxford Studies in Theological Ethics; Oxford: Oxford University Press, 2006), particularly ch. 1–3.

11 "The large-mouthed masks worn by the actors were so called from the resonance of the voice sounding through them; at any rate, in popular etymology." The derivation from *per* and *sonare* is given "[a]s if." So Walter W. Skeat, *An Etymological Dictionary of the English Language* (Oxford: Clarendon Press, 1879–82; repr., 1997), q.v. "Person."

12 The reader may recall that this Guide introduced ethics as entailing judgments made in any of these three persons. It is natural to us, as we move inductively into a humane subject, to recognize in it these three relationships. Even if we wish to eschew passing judgments upon others (in the third person), our face-to-face relationships may call for open speech, even if judgmental, with our friends (second person). And for the sake of minimizing self-deception, we cannot prescind categorically from first-person judgments upon ourselves.

13 As in Tooley, "Abortion and Infanticide."

14 Spaemann, *Persons*, 20.

15 Spaemann, *Persons*, 21.

16 This is Herbert McCabe's point in saying that God plus the universe do not make "two": the difference between creator and creature is

such that there is no frame of reference that can be drawn around them both. The creator is neither in the world nor outside the world. McCabe refers to the Jewish discovery of God as the creator as a new thing, unimagined by and unimaginable to the Greeks. The discovery is embodied in the Ten Commandments, which McCabe describes as "that great atheist manifesto," and which we can interpret as beginning, "Hear, O Israel, there are no gods!" Gods do not exist because they are, if anything, enslaving beings within the created world that need to be opposed; they are not, they cannot be, the creator, who is nothing in the created world. On this latter point, see McCabe, "The God of Truth," in his *God Still Matters*, 29–35 (32).

17 Spaemann, *Persons*, 25.

18 The text of the *Quicumque vult* can be found, among other places, in the U.S. Episcopal Church's 1979 Book of Common Prayer at pp. 864–5.

19 Robert W. Jenson, *On Thinking the Human: Resolutions of Difficult Notions* (Grand Rapids, Mich.: Eerdmans, 2003), 12; emphasis in original.

20 See *Summa theologiae* I.40.2, in the reply to the first objection: "The persons are the subsisting relations themselves."

BIBLIOGRAPHY

Listed here are all works cited in the notes, including the notes for further reading at the end of each chapter, excluding the Bible and classical references where no particular translation is quoted, and also excluding internet citations.

Abbott, Walter M. ed. *The Documents of Vatican II* (New York: Guild Press, 1966).

Achebe, Chinua, *Things Fall Apart* (New York: Anchor Books, 1994).

Apostle, Hippocrates G. trans. *Aristotle's Nichomachean Ethics* (Grinnell, Iowa: Peripatetic Press, 1984).

Aquinas, *The Summa Theologica of Saint Thomas Aquinas* (2 vols; trans. Fathers of the English Dominican Province, rev. Daniel J. Sullivan; Great Books of the Western World; Chicago: Encyclopaedia Britannica, 1950).

—*Selected Philosophical Writings* (selected and trans. Timothy McDermott; Oxford: Oxford University Press, 1993).

—*On Law, Morality, and Politics* (trans. Richard J. Regan; Indianapolis, Ind.: Hackett Publishing, 2nd edn, 2002).

Aristotle, *The Nicomachean Ethics* (trans. H. Rackham; Loeb Classical Library; Cambridge, Mass.: Harvard University Press, rev. edn, 1934).

Augustine, Saint, *St. Augustine's Confessions* (2 vols; trans. William Watts; Loeb Classical Library; Cambridge, Mass.: Harvard University Press, 1912).

—*Confessions* (trans. Henry Chadwick; Oxford: Oxford University Press, 1991).

Austin, Victor Lee, "John Paul II's Ironic Legacy in Political Theology," *Pro Ecclesia* 16 (2007): 165–94.

—*Up with Authority: Why We Need Authority to Flourish as Human Beings* (London: T & T Clark, 2010).

Bauby, Jean-Dominique, *The Diving-Bell and the Butterfly* (trans. Jeremy Leggatt; New York: Alfred A. Knopf, 1997).

Biggar, Nigel, *Aiming to Kill* (Cleveland, Ohio: Pilgrim Press, 2004).

—*Behaving in Public: How to Do Christian Ethics* (Grand Rapids, Mich.: Eerdmans, 2011).

Bonner, Gerald, *St. Augustine of Hippo: Life and Controversies* (Norwich: Canterbury Press, rev. edn, 1986).

Carlen, Claudia ed. *The Papal Encyclicals 1878–1903* (Wilmington, N.C.: McGrath, 1981).

Carmichael, E. D. H. (Liz), *Friendship: Interpreting Christian Love* (London: T & T Clark, 2004).

Charry, Ellen T., *God and the Art of Happiness* (Grand Rapids, Mich.: Eerdmans, 2010).

Cooper, David E. ed. *Ethics: The Classic Readings* (Oxford: Blackwell Publishers, 1998).

Curran, Charles E., and Richard A. McCormick (eds), *The Distinctiveness of Christian Ethics* (Readings in Moral Theology No. 2; New York: Paulist Press, 1980).

Davies, Brian, *The Thought of Thomas Aquinas* (Oxford: Clarendon Press, 1992).

Fitzgerald, Allan D. ed. *Augustine through the Ages: An Encyclopedia* (Grand Rapids, Mich.: Eerdmans, 2009).

Fletcher, Joseph, *Situation Ethics: The New Morality* (Philadelphia: Westminster Press, 1965).

Freedman, David Noel ed. *Eerdmans Dictionary of the Bible* (Grand Rapids, Mich.: Eerdmans, 2000).

Grotius, Hugo, *The Rights of War and Peace* (ed. Richard Tuck; 3 vols; Indianapolis, Ind.: Liberty Fund, 2005).

Gundry, Robert H., *Matthew* (Grand Rapids, Mich.: Eerdmans, 2nd edn, 1994).

Hart, David Bentley, *Atheist Delusions: The Christian Revolution and Its Fashionable Enemies* (New Haven: Yale University Press, 2009).

Hauerwas, Stanley, *Truthfulness and Tragedy* (Notre Dame, Ind.: University of Notre Dame Press, 1977).

—*A Community of Character* (Notre Dame, Ind.: University of Notre Dame Press, 1981).

Hemming, Laurence Paul, and Susan Frank Parsons (eds), *Restoring Faith in Reason: A New Translation of the Encyclical Letter* Faith and Reason *of Pope John Paul II Together with a Commentary and Discussion* (London: SCM Press, 2002).

Jenson, Robert W., *On Thinking the Human: Resolutions of Difficult Notions* (Grand Rapids, Mich.: Eerdmans, 2003).

Johnson, James Turner, *Morality and Contemporary Warfare* (New Haven: Yale University Press, 1999).

Kant, Immanuel, *The Fundamental Principles of the Metaphysic of Ethics* (trans. Otto Manthey-Zorn; New York: Appleton-Century, 1938).

Levenson, Jon D., *The Death and Resurrection of the Beloved Son: The*

Transformation of Child Sacrifice in Judaism and Christianity (New Haven: Yale University Press, 1993).

Loughlin, Stephen, "Thomas Aquinas and the Importance of Fasting to the Christian Life," *Pro Ecclesia* 17 (2008): 343–61.

MacIntyre, Alasdair, *After Virtue* (Notre Dame, Ind.: University of Notre Dame Press, 2nd edn, 1984).

"Mary: Grace and Hope in Christ. The Seattle Statement of the Anglican-Roman Catholic International Commission" (text with commentaries and study guide; ed. Donald Bolen and Gregory Cameron; London: Continuum, 2006).

Mattison, William C., III, *Introducing Moral Theology: True Happiness and the Virtues* (Grand Rapids, Mich.: Brazos Press, 2008).

McCabe, Herbert, *God Still Matters* (ed. Brian Davies; London: Continuum, 2003).

—*Law, Love, and Language* (Sheed and Ward, 1968; repr. London: Continuum, 2003).

—*God Matters* (Geoffrey Chapman, 1987; repr. London: Continuum, 2005).

—*The Good Life: Ethics and the Pursuit of Happiness* (ed. Brian Davies; London: Continuum, 2005).

McCoy, Alban, *An Intelligent Person's Guide to Christian Ethics* (London: Continuum, 2004).

Meilaender, Gilbert C., *Friendship: A Study in Theological Ethics* (Notre Dame, Ind.: University of Notre Dame Press, 1981).

Mill, John Stuart, *Utilitarianism* (ed. George Sher; Indianapolis, Ind.: Hackett Publishing, 2nd edn, 2001).

Miller, J. Michael ed. *The Encyclicals of John Paul II* (Huntington, Ind.: Our Sunday Visitor, 1996).

Newman, John Henry, *Parochial and Plain Sermons* (San Francisco: Ignatius Press, 1987).

Nouwen, Henri, *Adam: God's Beloved* (Maryknoll, N.Y.: Orbis Books, 1997).

O'Connell, Timothy E., *Principles for a Catholic Morality* (San Francisco: Harper and Row, rev. edn, 1990).

O'Donovan, Oliver, *The Just War Revisited* (Cambridge: Cambridge University Press, 2003).

—*The Ways of Judgment* (Grand Rapids, Mich.: Eerdmans, 2005).

—*Church in Crisis* (Eugene, Ore.: Cascade Books, 2008).

O'Donovan, Oliver, and Joan Lockwood O'Donovan, *Bonds of Imperfection* (Grand Rapids, Mich.: Eerdmans, 2004).

—(eds), *From Irenaeus to Grotius: A Sourcebook in Christian Political Thought* (Grand Rapids, Mich.: Eerdmans, 1999).

Pagden, Anthony, and Jeremy Lawrance (eds), *Vitoria: Political Writings* (Cambridge: Cambridge University Press, 1991).

Pieper, Josef, *The Four Cardinal Virtues* (Notre Dame, Ind.: University of Notre Dame Press, 1966).

Pinckaers, Servais, *The Sources of Christian Ethics* (trans. Mary Thomas Noble; Washington, D.C.: Catholic University of America Press, 1995).

—*Morality, The Catholic View* (South Bend, Ind.: St. Augustine's Press, 2003).

Polanyi, Michael, *Personal Knowledge: Towards a Post-Critical Philosophy* (Chicago: University of Chicago Press, corr. edn, 1962).

Pope, Stephen J. ed. *The Ethics of Aquinas* (Washington, D.C.: Georgetown University Press, 2002).

Porter, Jean, *The Recovery of Virtue: The Relevance of Aquinas for Christian Ethics* (Louisville, Ky.: Westminster/John Knox Press, 1990).

Raith, Charles, II, "Calvin's Critique of Merit, and Why Aquinas (Mostly) Agrees," *Pro Ecclesia* 20 (2011): 135–66.

Ramsey, Paul, *War and the Christian Conscience: How Shall Modern War Be Conducted Justly?* (Durham, N.C.: Duke University Press, 1961).

—*Deeds and Rules in Christian Ethics* (New York: Charles Scribner's Sons, 1967).

—*The Just War: Force and Political Responsibility* (New York: Charles Scriber's Sons, 1968).

Ratzinger, Joseph, *Church, Ecumenism, and Politics* (New York: Crossroad, 1988).

Reinders, Hans S., *Receiving the Gift of Friendship: Profound Disability, Theological Anthropology, and Ethics* (Grand Rapids, Mich.: Eerdmans, 2008).

Sacks, Oliver, *Seeing Voices: A Journey into the World of the Deaf* (Berkeley, Calif.: University of California Press, 1989; repr. New York: Vintage, 2000).

Schwartz, Daniel, *Aquinas on Friendship* (Oxford: Clarendon Press, 2007).

Skeat, Walter W., *An Etymological Dictionary of the English Language* (Oxford: Clarendon Press, 1879–82; repr., 1997).

Spaemann, Robert, *Basic Moral Concepts* (trans. T. J. Armstrong; London: Routledge, 1989).

—*Persons: The Difference between "Someone" and "Something"* (trans. Oliver O'Donovan; Oxford Studies in Theological Ethics; Oxford: Oxford University Press, 2006).

Sutton, Agneta, *Bioethics: A Guide for the Perplexed* (London: T & T Clark, 2008).

Teresa, Mother, *Where There Is Love, There Is God* (ed. Brian Kolodiejchuk; New York: Doubleday, 2010).

Tilley, Terrence W. ed. *New Horizons in Theology* (College Theology Society Annual Volume 50; Maryknoll, N.Y.: Orbis, 2005).

Tooley, Michael, "Abortion and Infanticide," *Philosophy and Public Affairs* 2 (1972): 37–65.

Wadell, Paul J., *Friendship and the Moral Life* (Notre Dame, Ind.: University of Notre Dame Press, 1989).

Walzer, Michael, *Just and Unjust Wars* (New York: Basic Books, 4th edn, 2006).

Weigel, George, *The End and the Beginning* (New York: Doubleday, 2010).

White, Thomas Joseph, "On the Universal Possibility of Salvation," *Pro Ecclesia* 17 (2008): 269–80.

Williams, Bernard, *Morality: An Introduction to Ethics* (New York: Harper & Row, 1972; repr. as Canto edn, Cambridge: Cambridge University Press, 1993).

Wright, N. T., *Surprised by Hope: Rethinking Heaven, Resurrection, and the Mission of the Church* (New York: HarperOne, 2008).

INDEX OF SCRIPTURAL REFERENCES

INDEX